GUINNESS WORLD RECORDS

Record-Breaking Comprehension
Year 6

Teacher's Book
Alison Milford

Published by
RISING★STARS
in association with

Rising Stars UK Ltd.
7 Hatchers Mews, Bermondsey Street, London, SE1 3GS
www.risingstars-uk.com

Every effort has been made to trace copyright holders and obtain their permission for the use of copyright materials. The author and publisher will gladly receive information enabling them to rectify any error or omission in subsequent editions. All facts are correct at the time of going to press. All referenced websites were correct at the time this book went to press.

Text, design and layout © Rising Stars UK Ltd.

The right of Alison Milford to be identified as the author of this work has been asserted by her in accordance with the Copyright, Design and Patents Act 1998.

Published 2013
Reprinted 2013 (twice), 2014
All underlying records data © Guinness World Records Ltd.

Published in association with Guinness World Records.

Author: Alison Milford
Text design: Burville-Riley Partnership/Words & Pictures Ltd
Typesetting: Words & Pictures Ltd
Cover design: Burville-Riley Partnership
Publisher: Becca Law
Project manager: Tracey Cowell
Editor: Jennie Clifford

Photo acknowledgements
Page 9: Emir Simsek/iStockphoto; **page 11**: © chieferu/iStockphoto; **page 15**: © Tribalium/iStockphoto; **page 17**: © COMMAND A DESIGN/iStockphoto; **page 19**: © enjoy industries/iStockphoto, Rosica Daskalova/iStockphoto; **page 21**: © blackred/iStockphoto; **page 25**: © Frank Ramspott/iStockphoto; **page 27**: © Bea Kraus/iStockphoto; **page 29**: © Nik Thavisone/iStockphoto; **page 31**: © pixitive/iStockphoto, © DimaChe/iStockphoto; **page 39:** © sceka/iStockphoto; **page 41**: © Linda Shannon/iStockphoto; **page 45**: © IdeaBug Media/iStockphoto; **page 47**: © klikk/iStockphoto; **page 51**: © chieferu/iStockphoto; **page 53**: © Lumumba/iStockphoto; **page 55**: © Yujin Somera/iStockphoto. **Rising Stars is grateful to Guinness World Records for supplying all of the record-related pictures in the book.**

All rights reserved. No part of this publication may be reproduced, stored in a retrieval system, or transmitted, in any form by any means, electronic, mechanical, photocopying, recording or otherwise, without the prior permission of Rising Stars.

British Library Cataloguing in Publication Data.
A CIP record for this book is available from the British Library.
ISBN: 978-0-85769-570-3

Printed by Ashford Colour Press

CONTENTS

How to use this book 4

Content summary grid 6

Most buildings climbed unassisted 8

Longest motorcycle ride through a tunnel of fire 10

Most expensive fungus species 12

Largest tug-of-war tournament 14

Largest revolving restaurant 16

Longest full-body-contact ice endurance 18

Youngest film director 20

Most tattooed person 22

Longest theatrical run 24

Most pots thrown in one hour by an individual 26

Longest rail grind on a snowboard 28

Greatest distance covered in 24 hours by wheelchair 30

Largest gathering of people dressed as Mohandas Gandhi 32

First gorilla born in captivity 34

Largest matchstick model 36

Largest violin 38

Largest concentration of geysers 40

Largest photo mosaic 42

Most consecutive foot-juggling flips 44

Largest panoramic painting 46

Longest time to live with a bullet in the head 48

Longest distance run full-body burn (without oxygen) 50

Oldest sculpture 52

Largest medicinal herb garden 54

Notes 56

GUINNESS WORLD RECORDS
RECORD-BREAKING COMPREHENSION – YEAR 6

HOW TO USE THIS BOOK

Record-Breaking Comprehension is a brand new resource that uses the appeal of Guinness World Records to engage pupils in reading comprehension texts.

The records are described via a range of fiction and non-fiction text types, including newspaper reports, instructional web pages, blog entries and letters. The grid on pages 6–7 summarises the text types covered.

This Teacher's Book provides:

- answers to the questions, plus guidance on AFs and question types covered;

- support and research pointers for the Beyond the Record activities;

- photocopiable activities for writing, speaking and listening, linked to each record.

Reading comprehension questions

The reading comprehension questions in the Pupil Book are split into three differentiated sections: On your marks, Get set and Go for gold! The questions within each section become increasingly more challenging. For Years 3 and 4, there are three questions in each section; this increases to four questions per section for Years 5 and 6. You may wish to ask different groups of children to answer a particular set, or sets, of questions, depending on their ability.

The questions cover a range of AFs and question types (literal, inference, deduction and personal opinion), details of which can be found with the answers. A summary of coverage can be found on the grid on pages 6–7.

Language activity worksheets

Each of the photocopiable activity worksheets focuses on different language features and skills that children need to develop within the year group, and includes grammar, spelling and punctuation activities.

There are suggestions for how to introduce each worksheet, as well as teaching prompts. A summary of the coverage for the worksheets can be found in the grid on pages 6–7.

Beyond the record

These follow-up activities can be used with any child, regardless of their level and progress through the reading comprehension questions. Many of the activities involve children researching more about the record and presenting their findings.

Each activity is accompanied by structured teacher's notes, including web references where appropriate. The activities can be used both for class work and homework.

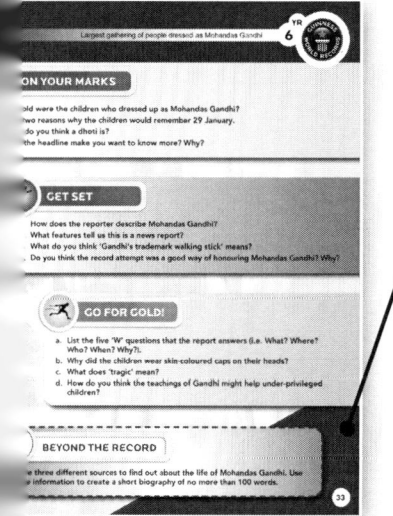

RECORD-BREAKING COMPREHENSION – YEAR 6

CONTENT SUMMARY GRID

Record title	Text type	AF coverage	Worksheet focus
Most buildings climbed unassisted	Letter: information	AF2, AF3, AF4, AF5, AF6	Formal language
Longest motorcycle ride through a tunnel of fire	Script: recount	AF2, AF3, AF5	Hyphens
Most expensive fungus species	Presentation notes: non-chronological report	AF2, AF3, AF4, AF5, AF6	Suffixes
Largest tug-of-war tournament	Online encyclopedia: non-chronological report	AF2, AF3, AF4, AF5	Adverbial phrases
Largest revolving restaurant	Restaurant review: recount	AF2, AF3, AF5, AF6	Informal and formal language
Longest full-body-contact ice endurance	Web page: biography	AF2, AF3, AF4, AF5, AF6	Synonyms
Youngest film director	Film review: biography	AF2, AF3, AF5, AF6	Persuasive language
Most tattooed person	Letter: recount	AF2, AF3, AF4, AF5, AF6	Thesaurus use
Longest theatrical run	Web page: non-chronological report	AF2, AF3, AF4, AF5, AF6	Active and passive voice
Most pots thrown in one hour by an individual	Magazine: recount/non-chronological report	AF2, AF3, AF4, AF5, AF6	Linking paragraphs
Longest rail grind on a snowboard	Magazine: recount	AF2, AF3, AF5, AF6	Homophones and other words that sound similar
Greatest distance covered in 24 hours by wheelchair	Web page: biography	AF2, AF3, AF4, AF5	Subjunctive verbs
Largest gathering of people dressed as Mohandas Gandhi	Newspaper: recount	AF2, AF3, AF4, AF5	Verb tenses

RECORD-BREAKING COMPREHENSION – YEAR 6

Record title	Text type	AF coverage	Worksheet focus
First gorilla born in captivity	Travel guide: non-chronological report	AF2, AF3, AF5, AF6	Proofreading text
Largest matchstick model	Magazine: recount/instructions	AF2, AF3, AF5, AF6	Using bullet points
Largest violin	Online encyclopedia: non-chronological report	AF2, AF3, AF4, AF5, AF6	Semicolons
Largest concentration of geysers	Encyclopedia: non-chronological report	AF2, AF3, AF4, AF5, AF6	Cohesion within texts
Largest photo mosaic	Web page: recount	AF2, AF3, AF4, AF5, AF6	Hyphens
Most consecutive foot-juggling flips	Newsletter: recount	AF2, AF3, AF4, AF5, AF6	Homophones
Largest panoramic painting	Magazine: recount/instructions	AF2, AF3, AF4, AF5, AF6	Proofreading text
Longest time to live with a bullet in the head	Magazine: biography	AF2, AF3, AF4, AF5, AF6	Expanded noun phrases
Longest distance run full-body burn (without oxygen)	Blog: recount	AF2, AF3, AF5, AF6	Adverbial phrases
Oldest sculpture	Online encyclopedia: non-chronological report	AF2, AF3, AF4, AF5, AF6	Colons
Largest medicinal herb garden	Magazine: non-chronological report	AF2, AF3, AF4, AF6	Suffixes

RECORD-BREAKING COMPREHENSION – YEAR 6

MOST BUILDINGS CLIMBED UNASSISTED

This text takes the form of a letters page from a newspaper. The letter and editorial relate to Alain Robert, who holds the Guinness World Record for the most buildings climbed unassisted.

Text type:	information/letter
AFs covered:	AF2, AF3, AF4, AF5, AF6
Specialist vocabulary:	unassisted, awe-inspiring, suction, vertigo, skyscraper, monument

ON YOUR MARKS

a. Alain comes from France. *Literal AF2*
b. Melina writes using informal language, such as 'awe-inspiring', 'I feel so lucky to have seen him. Keep climbing, "Spiderman"!' *Inference AF3, AF4, AF5*
c. Melina thinks Alain Robert is brave, courageous and inspirational. *Deduction AF3, AF6*
d. Personal opinion *AF3*

GET SET

a. Alain uses pipes and window frames to help him climb buildings. *Literal AF2*
b. Vertigo is a fear of heights – this could be a problem for Alain because he climbs such tall buildings. *Inference AF3*
c. Melina felt 'lucky' to see Alain because it's unusual to see someone climbing buildings with amazing skill and bravery. *Deduction AF3, AF5*
d. Personal opinion *AF2, AF3*

GO FOR GOLD!

a. Two adverbs used in the text are 'quickly' and 'confidently'. *Literal AF2, AF5*
b. Alain Robert has the nickname 'Spiderman' because he climbs up buildings like the superhero, Spiderman. *Inference AF3*
c. 'Solo urban climber' means a climber who climbs town or city buildings on their own. *Deduction AF3, AF5*
d. Personal opinion *AF2, AF3*

BEYOND THE RECORD

Use the internet to find out more about Alain 'Spiderman' Robert. Choose one of his record-breaking climbs and create a newspaper front-page report. Include a powerful headline, the who, what, why, when and where, and also reported and direct speech.

Background research, reading and discussion to help the children to prepare

- Guide children to websites to investigate, such as www.alainrobert.com/ (this website includes video clips).
- Show the children some of the newspaper reports about Alain Robert from online sources: see www.bbc.co.uk/news/world-middle-east-12888817.
- Discuss the features of a newspaper report.
- Talk about the audience for the report. Who will be their readers? How will this affect the way they write the report?

Recording their ideas

- Will the children make notes as they read text or watch video clips, or create a Mind Map™ with a branch for each of the five Ws?
- How will the children structure their information? With a framework of sub-headings, or one major heading and content split into paragraphs?
- Encourage the children to share their newspaper reports with other children in the class. Have all the news report features been covered? Is the headline catchy? Have they used reported and direct speech correctly?

LANGUAGE ACTIVITY WORKSHEET

- Use the worksheet to revise and extend skills in the features and language of formal letter writing. Read through the informal letter from the Pupil Book and discuss the features and language that make it informal. Discuss formal letter-writing features.
- Provide the children with the worksheet. Point out the word bank at the bottom of the page but encourage the children to use their own words and phrases too.
- Once they have completed the worksheet, encourage the children to share their letters. Do they follow a formal written style?

NAME: DATE:

OFFICIALLY AMAZING

CLIMBING THE CLOCK TOWER
Informal writing is personal and chatty.
Formal writing is impersonal and uses the third person.

A mayor from a local council has sent Alain Robert a formal letter to invite him to climb their town hall clock tower. Complete the letter using formal language. A word bank is given below to help you.

Milltown Council
Milltown Town Hall
Milltown
Millshire
MM1 1MM

29 March 2011

Dear Monsieur Robert

On behalf of Milltown Council, I am writing to express our sincere congratulations on your superb ascent of the Burj Khalifa tower in Dubai this week.

_____
_____
_____
_____
_____
_____
_____
_____

in my opinion	furthermore	in addition	rectify	extend
an invitation	in conclusion	your reply	Yours faithfully
sceptical	concerns	however	honour	majestic

RECORD-BREAKING COMPREHENSION – YEAR 6

LONGEST MOTORCYCLE RIDE THROUGH A TUNNEL OF FIRE

This recount text in the form of a television script is about Shabir Ahluwalia, who broke the Guinness World Record for the longest motorcycle ride through a tunnel of fire, in India on 13 March 2011.

Text type:	recount/script
AFs covered:	AF2, AF3, AF5
Specialist vocabulary:	extraordinary, death-defying, anti-inflammable, hazardous, feat, fearless

ANSWERS

ON YOUR MARKS

a. The three adjectives are 'wacky', 'extraordinary' and 'daring'. *Literal AF2, AF5*
b. Shabir wore a special mask to protect his face from the heat of the fire. *Inference AF3*
c. Shabir's motorbike needed to be powerful in order to drive quickly through the flaming tunnel. *Deduction AF3*
d. *Personal opinion AF2, AF3*

GET SET

a. Two descriptive words that mean dangerous are 'death-defying' and 'hazardous'. *Literal AF2, AF5*
b. There was 'a real sense of tension' because the record attempt could have gone wrong and Shabir might have been hurt. *Inference AF3*
c. The record attempt would need strict safety rules because driving through a tunnel of fire is very dangerous and there was a high risk of Shabir getting burned. *Deduction AF3*
d. *Personal opinion AF2, AF3*

GO FOR GOLD!

a. The phrase is: 'Shabir seems utterly fearless!' *Literal AF2*
b. Shabir's attempt was described as 'death-defying' because driving through a tunnel of fire could have killed him if it had gone badly wrong. *Inference AF3, AF5*
c. Shabir was 'racing at full speed' so he could get out of the tunnel of fire as quickly as he could before he started feeling the intense heat. *Deduction AF3, AF5*
d. *Personal opinion AF2, AF3*

BEYOND THE RECORD

On 10 August 2012 the Guinness World Record for the longest motorcycle ride through a tunnel of fire was broken by Andre De Kock and Enrico Schoeman in Vaalwater, Limpopo Province, South Africa. They rode a motorcycle and sidecar combination through a 103.09-m tunnel. Imagine that you are a TV presenter reporting on this record attempt. Write a short script about what you see. What language will you use to convey interesting information, excitement and tension?

Background research, reading and discussion to help the children to prepare

- Show a clip of the record attempt to the children. See multimedia.timeslive.co.za/videos/2011/03/sa-stuntmen-take-on-tunnel-of-fire/.
- Guide children to websites about the record, such as www.promotor.co.za/site/guinness-world-record-set-sa-photographer-motoring-scribe/.
- Use the text from the Pupil Book to study the features of a TV script. Point out the use of language and the short sentences.

Recording their ideas

- How will the children convert their notes into a TV script? Do they need support in finding more exciting vocabulary?
- Allow the children to read out their TV script while the film is rolling behind them.

LANGUAGE ACTIVITY WORKSHEET

- Point out the word *anti-inflammable* from the Pupil Book and ask the children what they think it means. Highlight the prefix *anti-* and explain this means *against*. Note the use of hyphens for prefixes that end in a vowel and where the root word starts with a vowel.
- Encourage the children to list more words using the hyphenated prefixes *anti-* and *co-*. Make sure the children have access to word banks and dictionaries.

Answers: Possible words include co-pilot, co-anchor, co-author, co-editor, co-exist; anti-oxidant, anti-aging, anti-hero, anti-aircraft.

NAME: DATE:

OFFICIALLY AMAZING

HOT HYPHENS!

Hyphens can be used to join a prefix to a root word, especially if the prefix ends with a vowel and the root word also begins with a vowel.

anti-inflammable, co-own, pre-eminent, re-enter

Write down hyphenated words that start with the prefix *anti-*.

_____

_____

_____

_____

Write down hyphenated words that start with the prefix *co-*.

_____

_____

_____

_____

Choose a word from each list and use it in an interesting sentence.

_____

_____

_____

_____

_____

_____

RECORD-BREAKING COMPREHENSION – YEAR 6

MOST EXPENSIVE FUNGUS SPECIES

This text is written as notes for a presentation on the white truffle, which holds the Guinness World Record for the most expensive fungus species.

Text type:	non-chronological report
AFs covered:	AF2, AF3, AF4, AF5, AF6
Specialist vocabulary:	species, fungus, truffle, organism, delicacy, precious

ON YOUR MARKS

a. Fungi grow in damp conditions. *Literal AF2*
b. Some chefs might lock white truffles in a safe because the truffles are so valuable and rare that they might be stolen. *Inference AF3*
c. Dogs and pigs can smell white truffles because they have a very strong sense of smell. *Deduction AF3*
d. *Personal opinion AF2, AF3, AF5, AF6*

GET SET

a. A white truffle is called the 'diamond of the table' because it is precious. *Literal AF2*
b. Dogs and pigs have to be 'trained' to find white truffles so that they can just focus on the smell and learn not to damage or eat the truffles as they dig them out. *Inference AF3*
c. There is an exclamation mark to emphasise how expensive white truffles are compared to white mushrooms. *Deduction AF3, AF4*
d. *Personal opinion AF2, AF3*

GO FOR GOLD!

a. White truffles are so expensive because they are very rare, they are hard to find and they are seen as a food delicacy. *Literal AF2, AF4*
b. 'Food delicacy' means a highly prized dish that is considered very special. *Inference AF3, AF5*
c. Chefs would only want to 'gently grate' a white truffle because its very strong taste and smell could be overpowering. It is also expensive, so a chef would not want to use a truffle all at once. *Deduction AF3, AF5*
d. *Personal opinion AF3, AF4, AF6*

BEYOND THE RECORD

Imagine you have just seen the white truffle presentation. Write down five questions to ask the presenter. Think carefully about the words you use. Use the text to find examples of truffle-related vocabulary.

Background research, reading and discussion to help the children to prepare

- Discuss with the children the difference between open and closed questions, and their uses.
- Talk about the type of questions that they could ask, e.g. more details about one area of information, a query about a fact or figure, a question about the presenter. Stress the importance of using truffle-related vocabulary.

Recording their ideas

- Will the children underline the text or use highlighters on areas of text that they want to ask questions about?
- How will they select the best questions and sequence them?
- Encourage the children to read out their questions. Have the children used the correct vocabulary? Are the answers already in the text?

Ideas for questions may include: other types of truffles, truffle eating in the past, how 'truffle hogs' are trained, what a white truffle looks and tastes like.

LANGUAGE ACTIVITY WORKSHEET

- Point out the *shus* sound to the children and encourage them to make the sound. Note the spelling patterns of the examples.
- Ask the children to turn the nouns into adjectives using the suffixes *-cious* and *-tious*. Ask them for the meaning of the nouns, followed by their adjectival meanings. The children then need to find and record the definitions of five *-cious* and *-tious* words, followed by one of their own choice.
- Before the end of the task, remind children of the spelling rules. Note that the word *anxious* has a different spelling despite the *shus* sound.

Answers: vicious, gracious, malicious, cautious, nutritious, ambitious.

NAME: DATE:

-CIOUS AND -TIOUS SUFFIXES

Root words (nouns) can be turned into adjectives by adding a suffix.
space → spac*ious*   infection → infect*ious*

Change the nouns on the truffles into adjectives using the suffixes -cious or -tious.

vice   grace   malice

_____   _____   _____

caution   nutrition   ambition

_____   _____   _____

Write down the definitions of these -cious and -tious adjectives.
Add one more at the bottom of the page.

1. delicious _____

2. precious _____

3. spacious _____

4. fictitious _____

5. suspicious _____

6. _____

RECORD-BREAKING COMPREHENSION – YEAR 6

LARGEST TUG-OF-WAR TOURNAMENT

This online encyclopedia entry provides information about tug of war and the Guinness World Record for the largest tug-of-war tournament.

Text type:	non-chronological report
AFs covered:	AF2, AF3, AF4, AF5
Specialist vocabulary:	opponent, strength, competitor, ceremonial, tournament

ON YOUR MARKS

a. The students from the Netherlands broke the Guinness World Record for the largest tug-of-war tournament. *Literal AF2*
b. The word 'grasp' means to take hold of something. *Inference AF3, AF5*
c. Sailors probably played tug of war as a way to build up strength for pulling the ropes on their ships. *Deduction AF3*
d. *Personal opinion AF3*

GET SET

a. Viking warriors used animal skin in tug of war instead of rope. *Literal AF2*
b. The 'heroic qualities' the Viking warriors were testing were strength, bravery and endurance. *Inference AF3*
c. The definition of 'tug of war' is at the beginning of the text so that the reader knows what tug of war is before they find out more about it. *Deduction AF3, AF4*
d. *Personal opinion AF2, AF3*

GO FOR GOLD!

a. Ancient cultures used tug of war for ceremonial rituals, as a strengthening exercise and as a competitive game. *Literal AF2*
b. Tug of war is a good 'strengthening exercise' because it uses leg and arm muscles. *Inference AF3*
c. When tug of war is played as a game, all ages can take part and the atmosphere is friendly and relaxed. When tug of war is played as a sport, the teams are much more competitive because they have practised before the event and want to win. *Deduction AF3*
d. *Personal opinion AF2, AF3*

BEYOND THE RECORD

Use the internet to find out the official rules of tug of war. Present this information as an easy-to-follow set of instructions aimed at someone who wants to take up the sport. Use bullet points, formal language, imperative verbs and sub-headings.

Background research, reading and discussion to help the children to prepare
- Guide children to websites such as www.tugofwar.co.uk and en.wikipedia.org/wiki/Tug_of_war.
- If possible, provide examples of rules for sports and games such as netball or football.
- Briefly revise the structural and language other features of an instruction text and discuss the different ways the children could present their instructions to make them easy to follow.

Recording their ideas
- How will the children present their set of instructions? On paper or using a design, word-processing or presentation tool on a computer, or tablet? Will they use colour and images?

Feedback: Encourage the children to share their instructions with each other. Did they use the right instructional structure and language? Which instructions worked well? Why?

LANGUAGE ACTIVITY WORKSHEET

- Use the worksheet to consolidate the children's skills on adverbial connective phrases.
- To complete the worksheet, the children must choose a suitable adverbial phrase from the table to complete the information text about the early history of football.
- Once they have completed the task, ask the children to read through the text. Do their choices work?

Possible answers: in fact, moreover, furthermore; however; such as, for example, namely, for instance; as a result, consequently, therefore; furthermore, in addition; such as, namely, specifically; As a consequence, as a result, consequently, in short; in contrast to, compared to; such as.

NAME: DATE:

FOOTBALL ADVERBIAL PHRASES

Adverbs can help us link our ideas in sentences and across paragraphs.

Use the table of adverbial words and phrases to help you fill in the gaps in the text below. In most cases, more than one answer is possible.

For ordering information	in the first place, to begin with, in addition, finally, then, after, next, lastly, firstly, secondly, thirdly
Adding extra information	furthermore, moreover, another thing, in addition, besides that, in fact, however
For summing up and results	overall, to summarise, to conclude, in conclusion, in short, for all these reasons, therefore, hence, consequently, thus, so, as a result
For examples	for example, for instance, in other words, namely, specifically, such as
For contrast	alternatively, however, in contrast to, on the other hand, compared to

Football is a very popular sport and is played by millions of people seriously and as a hobby. It is an ancient game, played by many cultures including the Ancient Greeks and Ancient Romans. _____ , some historians believe it was the Romans who introduced football to Britain during their occupation.

_____ , it wasn't until medieval times that the game became really popular. In some places it was called the 'mob game' because it usually involved a rowdy mob of people trying to get a ball over to the opposition's goal area in whatever way they could, _____ punching and kicking each other as violently as possible.

_____ , a national ban of the game was passed in 1342 by King Edward III so that men would stop fighting and causing rioting in the villages and towns. _____ he wanted them to stop playing so that they would spend more time concentrating on vital war skills training _____ archery and sword fighting.

_____ , football or the 'mob game' was not played openly for many years because of the ban but despite this, football was secretly still a popular game in many communities. Today, football is one of the few ancient games that is still played in Britain _____ others _____ Quarter-staff, which died out.

© Rising Stars UK Ltd. 2013   Record-Breaking Comprehension/Year 6/Largest tug-of-war tournament

RECORD-BREAKING COMPREHENSION – YEAR 6

LARGEST REVOLVING RESTAURANT

This restaurant review is for 'Bellini', in Mexico City, which holds the Guinness World Record for the largest revolving restaurant in the world.

Text type:	recount
AFs covered:	AF2, AF3, AF5, AF6
Specialist vocabulary:	revolving, circular, rotate, aroma, restaurant, diner

ON YOUR MARKS

a. Bellini is located on the 45th floor of the Mexico City World Trade Center. *Literal AF2*
b. The word 'all' is in bold to emphasise the large size of the revolving platform. *Inference AF3, AF5*
c. The writer seems excited and happy about going to the restaurant. *Deduction AF3, AF6*
d. *Personal opinion AF2, AF3*

GET SET

a. The sentence is: 'The dining and bar areas are all on a revolving platform that moves so slowly that it takes 1 hour, 45 minutes to rotate a full circle.' *Literal AF2*
b. The writer has added an exclamation mark to emphasise how amazing it is to be revolving and not feel dizzy. *Inference AF3, AF5, AF6*
c. 'Head-turning' is written in italics to emphasise its two meanings – a place where you turn your head as the restaurant revolves, and a place where you turn your head to see something because it is amazing. *Deduction AF3, AF5, AF6*
d. *Personal opinion AF2, AF3, AF6*

GO FOR GOLD!

a. Powerful adjectives in the text include airy, stunning, panoramic, overwhelming, thoughtful, gorgeous, delicious and romantic (any three answers are acceptable). *Literal AF2*
b. The writer creates a happy and contented atmosphere by using sensory imagery. She describes seeing the city in a 'gorgeous reddish glow', with twinkling street lights, and emphasises the smell of the 'delicious' food and the sound of the 'laughing' customers. *Inference AF3, AF5, AF6*
c. The writer is a bit 'overwhelmed' with the large size of the restaurant and its view when she arrives at Bellini. This feeling changes when she notices the 'thoughtful seating' and welcoming atmosphere for diners. *Deduction AF3*
d. *Personal opinion AF2, AF3, AF6*

BEYOND THE RECORD

Plan and write a review of a restaurant. Use a thesaurus to list powerful verbs and descriptive adjectives that could be included in the review.

Background research, reading and discussion to help the children to prepare

- Provide printed restaurant reviews from a selection of sources, and a thesaurus.
- Revise how to use a thesaurus. Explain how a text becomes more informative and interesting by using powerful verbs and descriptive adjectives.
- Discuss the features and layout of a restaurant review.

Recording their ideas

- The children could choose a real restaurant they have visited or a fictional one for their review.
- Will the children use a chosen layout with different information for each paragraph, use sub-headings, or write a straightforward recount of the visit?

Feedback: Encourage the children to share their reviews with others. Discuss how the review makes the reader want to visit or not visit the restaurant.

LANGUAGE ACTIVITY WORKSHEET

- Use the worksheet to revise the differences in formal and informal language.
- Ask the children to discuss and identify which phrases in the first restaurant review are informal.
- Once the children have created their own review, encourage them to swap work and discuss the vocabulary used. Is it a formal text?

Answers: coolest, walked in the door, mates, dead impressed, I got chilli and rice, steam coming out of my ears, Phew!, yummy, made by, down this way, come along.

NAME: DATE:

FORMAL AND INFORMAL RESTAURANT REVIEWS

Informal language is casual, as if you are speaking naturally.
Formal language is more official and polite.

Underline the informal words and phrases in this restaurant review.

Feb 2 February 2, 2012 21:12 GMT
Posted by Kate24

Joey's Grotto *****
I have just been to lunch at the coolest place in town, Joey's Grotto. As soon as I walked in the door with my mates, I was dead impressed by the feeling of the place: it really felt like a grotto! The walls looked like stone and everything was painted dark brown and bright red, with yellow seats and black tables. The food was even better. I got chilli and rice, which was so hot I felt the steam coming out of my ears. Phew! I ended my meal with a yummy sponge pud and custard made by Joey's mum. So, if you are ever down this way, come along to Joey's Grotto. It is a true five-star grotto treat.

Now rewrite the review using formal language: impersonal voice, formal vocabulary, polite language, formal connectives.

_____
_____
_____
_____
_____
_____
_____

RECORD-BREAKING COMPREHENSION – YEAR 6

LONGEST FULL-BODY-CONTACT ICE ENDURANCE

This web page-style information text is about Wim Hof, 'Iceman', who broke the Guinness World Record for longest full-body-contact ice endurance.

Text type:	information/biography
AFs covered:	AF2, AF3, AF4, AF5, AF6
Specialist vocabulary:	meditation, scientist, freezing, temperature, endurance, extreme

ON YOUR MARKS

a. Wim Hof is called the 'Iceman' because he does not feel the cold. *Literal AF2, AF3*
b. The snow would make most people's feet too cold and numb to be able to run. *Inference AF3, AF6*
c. The sub-headings are used to organise information and help readers to find information quickly. *Deduction AF3, AF4*
d. *Personal opinion AF3*

GET SET

a. Wim trains his body using meditation and exercise. *Literal AF2*
b. Scientists were baffled because Wim could cope with the extreme cold, unlike most people. *Inference AF3*
c. The bulleted list is used to show Wim's achievements clearly and to impress the reader with what he has done. *Deduction AF3, AF4, AF6*
d. *Personal opinion AF3*

GO FOR GOLD!

a. It is dangerous for most people to experience extreme cold because their body temperature would drop very low, resulting in possible death. *Literal AF2*
b. 'Meditation' means calmly thinking or concentrating on just one thing. *Inference AF3, AF5*
c. Wim only wears shorts to show that he does not feel the cold. *Deduction AF3*
d. *Personal opinion AF3*

BEYOND THE RECORD

Imagine that Wim Hof is planning to visit your school to talk about his ideas and achievements. Write a list of eight questions you would like to ask him.

Background research, reading and discussion to help the children to prepare

- Direct children to Wim Hof's website: www.icemanwimhof.com/en-home. If possible, watch a video clip of Wim-Hof running in the snow or sitting in a tank of ice. How do these video clips make the children feel?
- Provide science facts about the effects of the cold on the human body.

Recording their ideas

- How will the children record their ideas for questions? A simple list, sticky notes, or just single words initially?
- How will they select the best questions: in pairs, groups, or as a class?
- How will they sequence their questions?
- Can they team up with another pair or group to role-play the interview?

Ideas for questions may include: personal questions about his life, a memory, feelings or future plans.

LANGUAGE ACTIVITY WORKSHEET

- Use the worksheet to revise synonyms. You may wish to ask the children what an antonym is so that they can establish the difference between the two. The worksheet also gives the children the opportunity to extend their vocabulary.

- Encourage the children to use a thesaurus for this activity. Talk about the two different forms in which a thesaurus is available: in print and online. Which form is most appropriate for the work they are doing now? What about when working at home? Ask them to look up words associated with *cold* and *hot*. You may also wish to encourage them to look up *icy* and *warm*.

- Once they have created their poems, ask the children why they chose to use certain words. Discuss the difference that interesting vocabulary makes to a piece of writing.

Possible answers: *Cold*: chilly, freezing, icy, frosty, bitter, wintry, frozen, Arctic; *Hot*: warm, boiling, scorching, sizzling, searing, heated, burning, blistering, fiery, scalding.

NAME: DATE:

OFFICIALLY AMAZING

LONGEST FULL-BODY-CONTACT ICE ENDURANCE

Words that have the same or similar meanings are called **synonyms**. For example, 'cold' and 'chilly' are synonyms.

In the boxes below, list as many 'cold' and 'hot' synonyms as you can. You can use a thesaurus to help you.

COLD

HOT

Write a shape poem entitled 'Iceman' using words from both word banks.

© Rising Stars UK Ltd. 2013   Record-Breaking Comprehension/Year 6/Longest full-body-contact ice endurance

RECORD-BREAKING COMPREHENSION – YEAR 6

YOUNGEST FILM DIRECTOR

This film review for *Care of Footpath* provides information about Kishan Shrikanth, who broke the Guinness World Record for youngest film director.

Text type:	information/biography
AFs covered:	AF2, AF3, AF5, AF6
Specialist vocabulary:	triumph, debut, orphan, attitude underprivileged, director, dedicate, professionally

ANSWERS

ON YOUR MARKS

a. Kishan was the director, writer and star of *Care of Footpath*. *Literal AF2*
b. Kishan wanted to be a film director because he learned how to make films from an early age and wanted to use films to tell others about underprivileged children. *Inference AF3*
c. 'Against all odds' means that something is very unlikely to happen. *Deduction AF3, AF5*
d. *Personal opinion AF3, AF6*

GET SET

a. Some of the film community thought that Kishan's film was going to be 'childish' and 'amateurish'. *Literal AF2*
b. The school children called the boy an 'uneducated brute' because they assumed as an orphan living in the slums he had not been educated. *Inference AF3, AF5*
c. The 'aspects of film-making' that Kishan needed to learn included directing, camera work, acting, sound engineering, lighting and editing. *Deduction AF3*
d. *Personal opinion AF3*

GO FOR GOLD!

a. The review uses the phrases 'a triumph', 'beautifully acted', 'technically stunning' and 'immensely inspiring' (any two of these answers are acceptable). *Literal AF2*
b. The orphan boy could have changed attitudes towards slum children by showing that he had intelligence, ambition to get out of the slums and a good set of values. *Inference AF3*
c. 'Technically stunning' means that sound, camera angles and other technical aspects were used to create powerful images on film. *Deduction AF3, AF5*
d. *Personal opinion AF3*

BEYOND THE RECORD

Write a plan for a short film that will inspire underprivileged children to find a better life. Where does your film take place? Who is your main character? What happens? Present your ideas to the class.

Background research, reading and discussion to help the children to prepare

- Discuss why a film needs a plan before it can be filmed.
- Provide information about underprivileged children from online sources such as http://pankhudifoundation.org/, www.oxfam.org.uk/education and www.savethechildren.org.uk/if/the-issues.
- Discuss the main points and messages the children need to take into consideration for the film. Remind them that content needs to be concise and effective.

Recording their ideas

- What type of plan will the children create? Will they use a Mind Map™ or a storyboard?
- How will they present their plans: using Microsoft PowerPoint®, posters, a written framework and oral explanation?

Follow-up ideas: Perform the film in a drama session, using cameras or ICT applications. Give the children time to discuss and edit their film with a partner. Play the films for a class review.

LANGUAGE ACTIVITY WORKSHEET

- Use this worksheet to consolidate skills in using presentational devices to create effective text. Discuss the information needed for the press release, e.g. title, time, place, brief synopsis of the film, reviewer comments, persuasive words.
- The children should identify the information they will need from the Pupil Book and plan their press release on paper or on the computer.
- Encourage the children to share their drafts with a partner and then use the feedback to create the press release. Are the presentational devices and the language used effective?

NAME: DATE:

OFFICIALLY AMAZING

STOP PRESS!

A persuasive text tries to make the reader think, do or buy something.

Use the text from the Pupil Book to write a press release to persuade film reviewers to come and see *Care of Footpath* at your local cinema.

Use a range of presentational devices to make it as eye-catching and persuasive as possible: a catchy heading, sub-headings, underlining of words for emphasis, bullet points or lists.

RECORD-BREAKING COMPREHENSION – YEAR 6

MOST TATTOOED PERSON

This informal letter is written from the perspective of a teenager. She recounts her visit to a local arts festival where she sees Lucky Diamond Rich, who holds the Guinness World Record for the most tattooed person.

Text type:	recount/informal letter
AFs covered:	AF2, AF3, AF4, AF5, AF6
Specialist vocabulary:	unicycle, tattoo, chainsaw, temporary, pattern, permanent, attached

ANSWERS

ON YOUR MARKS

a. Maya saw Lucky Diamond Rich at a local arts festival in Australia. *Literal AF2*
b. Maya's mum was worried Lucky might get hurt during the juggling act because it looked dangerous. *Inference AF3*
c. It is an informal letter because Maya writes it as if she is talking directly to her friend, using informal phrases. *Deduction AF3, AF4, AF5*
d. *Personal opinion AF3*

GET SET

a. Informal phrases include 'without a doubt', 'I couldn't take my eyes off him', 'By the way', 'Lucky is so cool', 'Gotta go now', 'See you soon' (any two of these answers are acceptable). *Literal AF2, AF5*
b. Lucky Diamond Rich has started to use white tattoos so that they will stand out over the bluey-black ones. *Inference AF3*
c. Lucky isn't worried about what people think about him because he has a lot of confidence and likes the way the tattoos make him look different. *Deduction AF3*
d. *Personal opinion AF3, AF6*

GO FOR GOLD!

a. Maya noticed that all of Lucky's teeth were silver. *Literal AF2*
b. Maya wrote a letter because she had so much to say about Lucky Diamond Rich and it wouldn't have fitted on a postcard. *Inference AF3, AF6*
c. Lucky performs at arts festivals because the festivalgoers are likely to enjoy seeing him perform his juggling act and to admire his tattoos. *Deduction AF3*
d. *Personal opinion AF3*

BEYOND THE RECORD

Choose two sources to help you research and create a short biography about the life of Lucky Diamond Rich. Include an opening introductory paragraph, information about his life and a closing paragraph summarising what you think of him.

Background research, reading and discussion to help the children to prepare

- Print out texts from online interviews, e.g. www.smh.com.au/news/National/Sydneys-Lucky-Diamond/2004/12/15/1102787149631.html (websites may not be suitable for children to view independently due to inappropriate advertising).
- If possible, watch an interview with Lucky Diamond Rich: www.youtube.com/watch?v=Vu1BJH52x3s.
- Discuss the features of a biographical text. Emphasise the need to make sure that facts and quotes are correct when writing a biography.

Recording their ideas

- How will children put the information together? Will they use bullet points or sub-headings? If it is a filmed or recorded biography, will they write out the script first?

Feedback: Encourage the children to share their completed biographies. Do they have the features of biographical texts? Is there a clear introduction and ending?

LANGUAGE ACTIVITY WORKSHEET

- Use the worksheet to consolidate skills in using a thesaurus. Explain how a thesaurus can help develop a more adventurous vocabulary.
- Encourage the children to discuss particular words they like and could use in future work.
- Once the children have rewritten the passage, let them compare their different versions and identify how the text changes as a result of wider vocabulary use.

NAME: DATE:

OFFICIALLY AMAZING

THESAURUS TATTOOS

A thesaurus gives us a wide and varied selection of words that have a similar meaning (synonyms).

It can help you develop a more effective and imaginative vocabulary.

Use a thesaurus to write down three words that have the same meaning as those below.

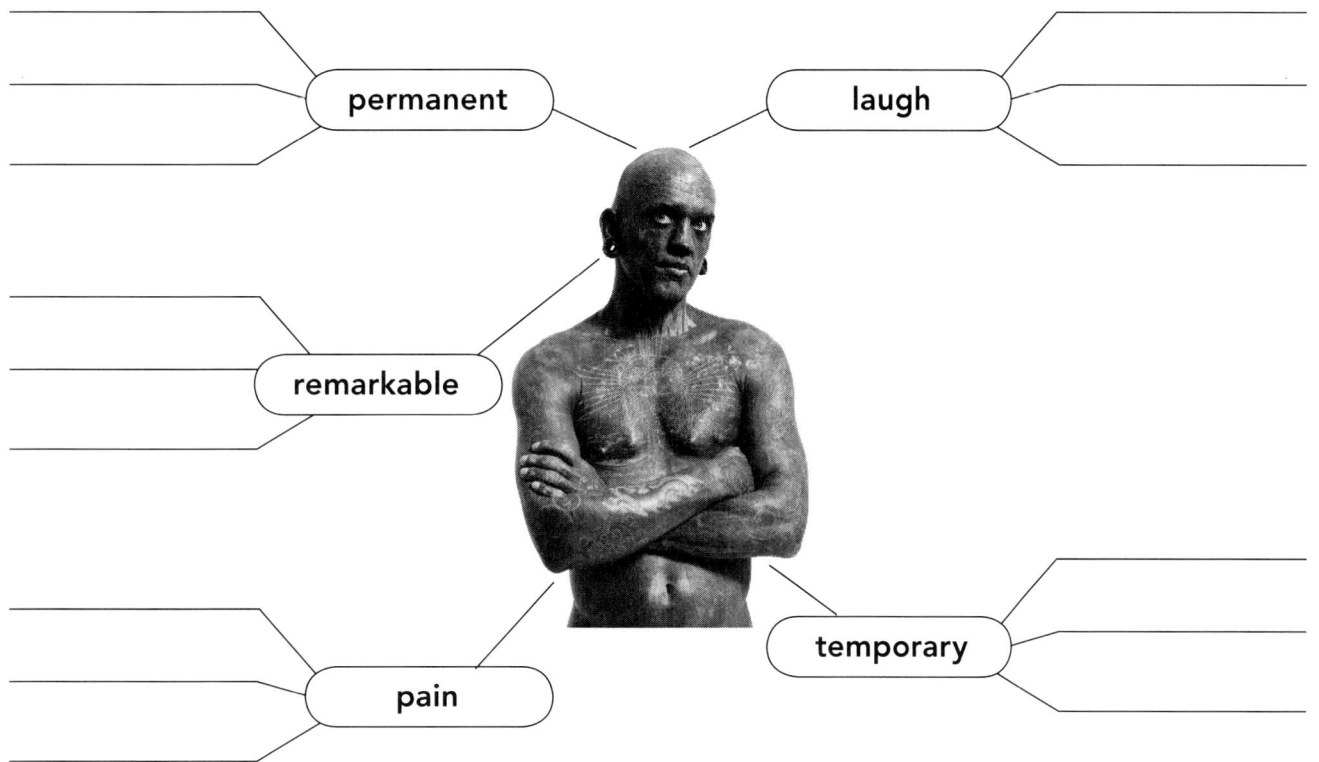

On a separate piece of paper, rewrite the passage below using a thesaurus to help you change some of the vocabulary. How different can you make it?

> The young man turned off the dark lane and walked wearily towards the large rambling house that loomed out above the trees. With a shiver, he knocked on the rotting wooden door and waited patiently. He knew it would open eventually: he had been asked to come. He looked at his dinner invitation with a drawing of a lamb on it; just like the tattoo on his arm. Suddenly, the door began to slowly and steadily creak open.
>
> 'You've come at last,' said a high voice. 'I was getting hungry.'
>
> Looking at the smooth hand that grabbed him around the neck, the man cried in horror as he saw the snarling tattoo of a wolf.

© Rising Stars UK Ltd. 2013

RECORD-BREAKING COMPREHENSION – YEAR 6

LONGEST THEATRICAL RUN

This web page details the history and plot of the West End play, *The Mousetrap*, which holds the Guinness World Record for the longest theatrical run.

Text type:	recount
AFs covered:	AF2, AF3, AF4, AF5, AF6
Specialist vocabulary:	anniversary, theatrical, legendary, durable, adapted, mystery, suspense

ANSWERS

ON YOUR MARKS

a. *The Mousetrap* was first staged at the Ambassadors Theatre in London's West End. *Literal AF2*
b. Theatregoers are asked not to reveal the identity of the murderer because it would spoil the mystery and ending for others who have not seen the play. *Inference AF3*
c. An understudy takes over a role if an actor is ill or away. *Deduction AF3*
d. Personal opinion *AF3, AF5, AF6*

GET SET

a. The three Guinness World Records mentioned in the web page are the world's longest theatrical run; the most durable West End actor; the world's longest-serving understudy. *Literal AF2*
b. A diamond anniversary celebrates 60 years. *Inference AF3*
c. The plot is short summary to encourage the reader to go to watch the play to find out what happens. *Deduction AF3, AF4, AF6*
d. Personal opinion *AF3*

GO FOR GOLD!

a. The adjective used to mean 'famous' is 'legendary'. *Literal AF2, AF5*
b. The radio play would need adapting for the theatre so that it could include physical action. *Inference AF3*
c. The country hotel is cut off by snow so that all the main characters are in the same place at the time of the murder, increasing the suspense about the identity of the murderer. *Deduction AF3, AF6*
d. Personal opinion *AF3, AF4, AF6*

BEYOND THE RECORD

Use at least two sources to help you to write a short biography of Dame Agatha Christie that could be published in a theatre programme for *The Mousetrap*.

Background research, reading and discussion to help the children to prepare

- Provide information about Dame Agatha Christie or guide children to websites such as www.agathachristie.com/ and http://agathachristie.wikia.com/wiki/Agatha_Christie.
- If possible, provide a selection of theatre programmes with short biographies of the playwright and actors.
- Explain that a biography for a theatre programme must be concise, and every word must count. Note that only the main relevant events are recorded.

Recording their ideas

- Discuss how the children will record their biographies: highlighted text, Mind Maps™, bullet points, sticky notes, etc.
- What information will they include in their biography? Why?
- Ask the children to check their work to see if it includes the correct biographical features.

Ideas may include: Agatha Christie's full name, when and where she was born, how many novels and theatrical plays she wrote, what genre she is famous for, her death, her enduring popularity.

LANGUAGE ACTIVITY WORKSHEET

- This worksheet can be used to investigate the effect of a passive voice in a text. Point out the examples at the top of the page. If necessary, give some more examples until the children are confident about the idea of passive and active voice.
- Discuss how there is a different emphasis when the whodunnit alibis have a passive voice compared to an active voice.
- Point out the use of a passive voice in other texts, e.g. formal language texts.

Answers: 1. The croquet lawn was mowed by Jacob. 2. The pet snake was fed by Colonel Plant. 3. A long letter was written by Lady West. 4. Lord West's shoes were polished by Johnson, the butler. 5. The medicine cabinet was checked by Millie. 6. Johnson, the butler, was arrested by Detective Gaskin for the murder of Lord West.

NAME: DATE:

PASSIVE VOICE – WHODUNNIT ALIBIS

We can change the effect and emphasis of a sentence by using a passive voice instead of an active voice.

Active voice: John (main subject) washed (main verb) up the dishes (something else).

Passive voice: The dishes (something else) were washed (main verb) up by John (main subject).

Turn these active-voice alibis of murder-mystery suspects into passive-voice sentences.

1. Jacob was mowing the croquet lawn.

_____

2. Colonel Plant was feeding his pet snake.

_____

3. Lady West was writing a long letter.

_____

4. Johnson, the butler, was polishing Lord West's shoes.

_____

5. Millie was checking her medicine cabinet.

_____

6. Detective Gaskin was arresting Johnson, the butler, for the murder of Lord West.

_____

RECORD-BREAKING COMPREHENSION – YEAR 6

MOST POTS THROWN IN ONE HOUR BY AN INDIVIDUAL

This arts and crafts magazine article is about Mark Byles who, on 29 June 2009, broke the Guinness World Record for the most pots thrown in one hour by an individual.

Text type:	recount/instructions
AFs covered:	AF2, AF3, AF4, AF5, AF6
Specialist vocabulary:	pottery, mould, ceramics, individual, competition, thrown

ON YOUR MARKS

a. Mark Byles 'threw' flowerpots to break the record. *Literal AF2*
b. The competition might have been 'thrilling' because the potters were trying to beat each other by throwing the most pots in one hour. *Inference AF3, AF5*
c. The guidelines are in a bulleted list so that each rule is clear to read. *Deduction AF3, AF4, AF6*
d. *Personal opinion AF2, AF3*

GET SET

a. Two adjectives that describe Mark Byles' flowerpots are 'extraordinary' and 'perfect'. *Literal AF2, AF5*
b. There are strict guidelines for this Guinness World Record to make sure that it is fair for anyone wanting to break the record. *Inference AF3, AF4, AF6*
c. The writer thinks Mark's pottery skills are very good because he/she says that Mark has skill and patience 'in abundance' and describes his pots as 'extraordinary' and 'perfect'. *Deduction AF3, AF5*
d. *Personal opinion AF2, AF3, AF6*

GO FOR GOLD!

a. The other word used in the text which means 'pottery' is 'ceramics'. *Literal AF2, AF5*
b. The guidelines insist on flowerpots because they are a familiar shape for most people, so an easier pot to make. *Inference AF3*
c. A pottery expert was needed to check the flowerpots because they know what to look for in a perfect pot. *Deduction AF3*
d. *Personal opinion AF2, AF3*

BEYOND THE RECORD

Use printed and internet sources to help you create an instruction text on 'How to throw a clay pot' for people keen to learn how to do it. Think about how you will lay out the instructions and information so that the text is easy to follow, for example using bulleted lists, labelled diagrams and instructional language.

Background research, reading and discussion to help the children to prepare

- Provide relevant craft books, instruction leaflets and access to websites such as http://pottery.about.com/od/throwingprojects/ss/bascylinder_all.htm and www.monkeysee.com/play/9069-how-to-throw-clay-on-a-pottery-wheel.
- Discuss the features of instructional texts.

Recording their ideas

- Encourage the children to make notes on how to throw a clay pot from the sources they have chosen.
- How have they decided to present their instructions? A short instruction leaflet, a Microsoft PowerPoint® presentation, a poster?
- Ask the children to discuss their instructions with others and highlight the instructional features and language they used.

LANGUAGE ACTIVITY WORKSHEET

- Use the worksheet to consolidate skills in creating cohesion within a text. Point to the information at the top of the page. Discuss the two different devices and why it is important to have links throughout a text.
- The children should read through the text, underlining the linking devices that have been outlined at the top of the worksheet.
- Once they have completed the worksheet, encourage the children to check each other's work to see if they have underlined the correct links.

Answers: Tea, teapot, However, teapot, China, China, teapot, Furthermore, tea, In addition, China, teapot, tea, teapot, tea, tea, tea, teapots, teapots, Consequently.

NAME: DATE:

OFFICIALLY AMAZING

POT PARAGRAPHS

When writing paragraphs, the information and topic subject in each paragraph need to be linked throughout the text. To do this, we use devices such as:
- repeating a word or phrase relating to the text subject
- using connectives.

Read through the information report below and underline the linking devices used.

China's teapot triumphs

Fancy a cup of tea? Then you may need a teapot. However, you won't want one as big as the Guinness World Records' largest ceramic teapot, which was made in China in February 2006. Designed and made by Sanbao Xu, in Yixing, Jiangsu Province, China, the massive teapot is made from purple sand and is 1.8 m high and 1.5 m in diameter. Furthermore, it can hold an incredible 10 kg of tea at one time.

In addition to the world's largest teapot, China is also home to the world's largest teapot monument or building. If you travel to the town of Meitan, you will come across their famous tea museum, which is shaped like a huge clay teapot. With a diameter of 24 metres, it looks like it should hold gallons of tea, but on closer inspection visitors soon realise that it is actually the museum building itself. It even has a smaller building shaped like a tea cup!

Both Meitan and Yixing have strong connections with tea and teapots. Meitan is famous for its Chinese green tea and the town of Yixing is well known for the manufacture of teapots. Consequently, it is not surprising they have both created two record-breaking teapots.

GUINNESS WORLD RECORDS

RECORD-BREAKING COMPREHENSION – YEAR 6

LONGEST RAIL GRIND ON A SNOWBOARD

This magazine article is about how Calum Paton and how, on 2 December 2012, he set the Guinness World Record for the longest rail grind on a snowboard.

Text type:	recount
AFs covered:	AF2, AF3, AF5, AF6
Specialist vocabulary:	snowboard, grind, enthusiast, manoeuvred, triumph, challenge

ANSWERS

ON YOUR MARKS

a. The event was organised to give UK snowboarders the chance to try to break the existing world record. *Literal AF2*
b. The phrase 'as if he was locked onto the rail' means that he looked as if he was well balanced on the rail and was not going to fall off. *Inference AF3, AF5*
c. The event was held indoors because there usually isn't enough snow in the UK for snowboarding. *Deduction AF3*
d. *Personal opinion AF3, AF6*

GET SET

a. Calum 'manoeuvred' his snowboard on the rail 'confidently'. *Literal AF2*
b. The rail had to be custom built so that it would fit into the venue and be the right length for the Guinness World Record attempt. *Inference AF3*
c. People were packing up before the end of the event because they thought that there would be no more successful attempts at the record. *Deduction AF3*
d. *Personal opinion AF2, AF3*

GO FOR GOLD!

a. The attempts were 'frustrating' because they all fell short of the distance needed to break a new record. *Literal AF2*
b. The phrase 'totally stoked' means very happy, excited or exhilarated. *Inference AF3, AF5*
c. The article is meant for snowboard enthusiasts because it uses snowboarding terms and is written by an enthusiast who conjures up the importance and excitement of the day using appropriate vocabulary. The article is also from a magazine that focuses on snow and ice sports. *Deduction AF3, AF5, AF6*
d. *Personal opinion AF2, AF3*

BEYOND THE RECORD

Use books and the internet to help you compile a 10-term glossary of snowboard moves and tricks. Consider the layout. Think about using sub-headings, easy-to-read captions, diagrams and pictures.

Background research, reading and discussion to help the children to prepare
- Discuss what a glossary is and where one is usually found.
- Provide examples of glossaries (in print and online) and access to websites such as www.abc-of-snowboarding.com/snowboarding-tricks/ and www.adventuresportsonline.com/snowboardglossary.htm.

Recording their ideas
- Encourage the children to think about where their glossary will be used, e.g. on a website, in a snowboarding manual, a book, a magazine, on a poster at a snowboarding venue, etc.
- Will the glossary be written by hand, on the computer, or a mix of both? How will the children add in diagrams, pictures or photographs?
- How will the children set out their glossary: alphabetically or by topic?

Feedback: Encourage the children to share their glossaries with others. What could be added or improved?

LANGUAGE ACTIVITY WORKSHEET

- This worksheet focuses on words that sound the same or similar. Point out the definition at the top of the page. Discuss the rule that *-ce* endings give the noun and *-se* endings give the verb.
- Ask the children to cross out the incorrect word in the sentences and write out the definitions of the eight words. Can they think of a strategy for remembering which spelling is for the noun and which is for the verb?

Answers: advice, licensed, practise, prophecy.

OFFICIALLY AMAZING

WORDS THAT SOUND THE SAME OR SIMILAR

Some words sound the same or similar but are spelled differently and have different meanings.

For some words that sound the same or similar, the nouns end in -ce and the verbs end in -se.

Cross out the incorrect word in the sentences below.

Becky took advise/advice from her coach to perform a half-pipe turn.

Leroy was licenced/licensed to use the top slopes.

To attempt the 50/50 grind, Chloe had to practice/practise everyday.

There was a prophecy/prophesy that UK snowboarders would win.

Write the definitions for the words below and indicate whether they are nouns (n) or verbs (v).

Glossary

advice: (n) _____

advise: (v) _____

licence: _____

license: _____

practice: _____

practise: _____

prophecy: _____

prophesy: _____

© Rising Stars UK Ltd. 2013   Record-Breaking Comprehension/Year 6/Longest rail grind on a snowboard

RECORD-BREAKING COMPREHENSION – YEAR 6

GREATEST DISTANCE COVERED IN 24 HOURS BY WHEELCHAIR

This web page-style biographical text is about Mário Trindade, who broke the Guinness World Record for the greatest distance covered in 24 hours by wheelchair.

Text type:	biography
AFs covered:	AF2, AF3, AF4, AF5
Specialist vocabulary:	diagnosed, scoliosis, surgery, miracle, disability, marathon, exercise

ON YOUR MARKS

a. Scoliosis is a condition that causes a curve in the spine. *Literal AF2*
b. The word 'miracle' means something that happens that is seemingly impossible. *Inference AF3, AF5*
c. The text is a biography. It retells the life, in chronological order, of Mário Trindade. *Deduction AF3, AF4*
d. *Personal opinion AF2, AF3*

GET SET

a. The adjective used to describe Mário's operation is 'unsuccessful'. *Literal AF2, AF5*
b. Playing basketball helped Mário because it gave him something positive to focus on. He also realised that he could have an active life in a wheelchair. *Inference AF3*
c. Mário 'chose' the wheelchair because the chance of a successful operation was very small. *Deduction AF3*
d. *Personal opinion AF2, AF3*

GO FOR GOLD!

a. Mário's three inspirational qualities are his 'determination', 'commitment' and 'courage'. *Literal AF2*
b. The two choices after his operation gave Mário 'the hardest decision of his life' because he had to choose between taking the very slim chance of walking again or spending the rest of his life in a wheelchair. *Inference AF3*
c. Mário uses an adapted racing wheelchair because it needs to move very quickly and be durable enough for long marathons. *Deduction AF3*
d. *Personal opinion AF2, AF3*

BEYOND THE RECORD

Mário Trindade started his world record attempt on 3 December 2007, the International Day of People with Disabilities. He did this to show what disabled athletes can do and achieve. Use two sources to research three different sports of the Paralympics. Create a poster for one of the events and use persuasive text to encourage people to come and support it.

Background research, reading and discussion to help the children to prepare

- Collect and provide printed information and online videos about the 2012 Paralympics. Guide the children to websites such as www.paralympic.org/ and www.paralympics.org.uk/.
- Emphasise the importance of knowing who their audience might be.

Recording their ideas

- How will the children make their designs eye-catching? Using headings, clear fonts, bullet points, logos?
- What kind of text and language will the children use? Catchphrases, facts (what, where, when, why, who), persuasive language, rhetorical questions?

Feedback: Ask the children to present their posters and discuss who they were aimed at, how they planned them, and why they chose the designs, slogans and language. What could be improved?

LANGUAGE ACTIVITY WORKSHEET

- This worksheet can be used to investigate the effect of a passive voice in a text. Point out the examples given at the top of the page. If necessary, give some more examples until the children are confident about the idea of passive and active voice.
- Discuss how there is a different emphasis when the sporting statements have a passive voice compared to an active voice.
- Point out the use of a passive voice in other texts, e.g. formal language texts.

Answers: Thomas won the gold medal for the 100-m sprint; Volunteers removed the athletes' kit bags from the track; Everyone in the stadium sang the national anthem of Great Britain; On-site vendors sold hot food and drink; Children in the crowd waved flags; An event official measured the long jump.

NAME: **DATE:**

OFFICIALLY AMAZING

ACTIVE AND PASSIVE VOICE

We can change the effect and emphasis of a sentence by using a passive voice instead of an active voice.

Active voice: Anna (main subject) won (main verb) the race (something else).

Passive voice: The race (something else) was won (main verb) by Anna (main subject).

Turn these passive-voice descriptions of sporting performances into active-voice sentences.

1. The gold medal for the 100-m sprint was won by Thomas.

_____

2. The athletes' kit bags were removed from the track by volunteers.

_____

3. The national anthem of Great Britain was sung by everyone in the stadium.

_____

4. Hot food and drink were sold by on-site vendors.

_____

5. Flags were waved by children in the crowd.

_____

6. The long jump was measured by an event official.

_____

© Rising Stars UK Ltd. 2013   Record-Breaking Comprehension/Year 6/Greatest distance covered in 24 hours by wheelchair

GUINNESS WORLD RECORDS

RECORD-BREAKING COMPREHENSION – YEAR 6

LARGEST GATHERING OF PEOPLE DRESSED AS MOHANDAS GANDHI

This news report is about a group of underprivileged children who broke the Guinness World Record for the largest gathering of people dressed as Mohandas Gandhi.

Text type:	recount
AFs covered:	AF2, AF3, AF4, AF5
Specialist vocabulary:	peace, spiritual, Mohandas Gandhi, assassinated, remembrance, dhoti

ON YOUR MARKS

a. The children who dressed up as Mohandas Gandhi were aged between 10 and 16. *Literal AF2*
b. The children would remember 29 January because it is the date when Gandhi was assassinated and the date they broke a Guinness World Record. *Inference AF3*
c. A dhoti is a piece of clothing that covers the body below the waist. *Deduction AF3*
d. *Personal opinion AF2, AF3*

GET SET

a. The reporter describes Mohandas Gandhi as 'one of India's greatest spiritual leaders'. *Literal AF2, AF5*
b. This is a news report because it has the newspaper's name and date at the top, a headline, informative sentences answering the five Ws and the name of the reporter. *Inference AF3, AF4*
c. 'Gandhi's trademark walking stick' means that Gandhi was well known for carrying a walking stick. *Deduction AF3, AF5*
d. *Personal opinion AF2, AF3*

GO FOR GOLD!

a. What?: a half-kilometre peace march; Where?: through the centre of Kolkata, India; Who?: 485 underprivileged children; When?: 29 January 2012; Why?: to remember Mohandas Gandhi. *Literal AF2*
b. The children wore skin-coloured caps on their heads to look like Gandhi, who was bald. *Inference AF3*
c. The word 'tragic' means terribly sad. *Deduction AF3, AF5*
d. *Personal opinion AF2, AF3*

BEYOND THE RECORD

Use three different sources to find out about the life of Mohandas Gandhi. Use the information to create a short biography of no more than 100 words.

Background research, reading and discussion to help the children to prepare

- Provide any relevant books and guide children to websites such as www.thebiographychannel.co.uk/biographies/mohandas-gandhi.html and www.history.com/topics/mahatma-gandhi.
- Briefly go through the features of a biography. Discuss the length of the biography that the children need to write and how they need to record important facts and events concisely.

Recording their ideas

- How will the children choose the most important facts and information for their short biographies? Through discussion, elimination of less important information, rewriting sentences to be more concise?
- How will the biographies be presented? As a short fact file with sub-headings and colons, as short paragraphs, as a timeline with photos and captions?

Feedback: Encourage the children to share their biographies. Are they easy to read, do they contain biographical features and cover Gandhi's life? What could be improved?

LANGUAGE ACTIVITY WORKSHEET

- This worksheet allows revision of the correct and consistent use of verb tenses in a piece of writing. Provide the children with the worksheet and explain that some of the verb tenses are wrong. It is their job to act as a proofreader and correct any errors.
- Ask the children not to look at the text in the Pupil Book until they have finished.
- When the children are confident they have found all the mistakes, they should self-mark their work using the text from the Pupil Book.

Answers: take/took, is/was, break/broke, is/was, carry/carried, wear/wore, will come/came, helped/helps, teach/taught, wants/wanted.

TENSES TROUBLE

Verbs can be written in the **past**, **present** or **future** tense.

Ten of the verb tenses in this newspaper report are incorrect. Proofread the text and correct the mistakes. Don't look at the original text until you have checked your work!

WORLD RECORD FOR GANDHI PEACE MARCH

Yesterday, 485 under-privileged children, aged between 10 and 16, take part in a half-kilometre peace march through the centre of Kolkata. They were walking in remembrance of one of India's greatest spiritual leaders, Mohandas Gandhi, who is tragically assassinated on that date, 64 years ago.

The marching youngsters also successfully break the Guinness World Record for the largest gathering of people dressed as Mohandas Gandhi.

Usha Gokani, Gandhi's granddaughter, is among the watching crowds as hundreds of Mohandas Gandhis, wearing identical grey moustaches, round glasses, white traditional Indian dhotis and shawls, walked together as part of the 'Rise Up' peace march. The children carry Gandhi's trademark walking stick and wear skin-coloured caps on their heads.

The idea for the 'Rise Up' peace march will come from a small charity called TRACKS (Training Resources and Care For Kids). The charity helped single mothers and children who live in the train stations and streets of Mumbai by providing much-needed health care and advice. Before the event, charity workers teach the children about Gandhi so they could learn more about how he wants to improve the lives of Indian people through peaceful actions.

RECORD-BREAKING COMPREHENSION – YEAR 6

FIRST GORILLA BORN IN CAPTIVITY

This travel-guide page provides tourist information about Columbus Zoo and Aquarium, and Colo the gorilla, who holds two Guinness World Records: the first gorilla born in captivity and the oldest living gorilla in captivity.

Text type:	non-chronological report
AFs covered:	AF2, AF3, AF5, AF6
Specialist vocabulary:	aquarium, gorilla, captivity, conservation, endangered, species

ANSWERS

ON YOUR MARKS

a. Colo was born at Columbus Zoo and Aquarium in Powell, Ohio, USA. *Literal AF2*
b. The zoo might have donation boxes to help raise money for the conservation programme. *Inference AF3*
c. You would find the Queensland koalas in the Australia zone. *Deduction AF3*
d. *Personal opinion AF2, AF3*

GET SET

a. Visitors can find out more about endangered species by reading the information provided with the exhibits. *Literal AF2*
b. It is 'incredible' that Colo holds two records because you wouldn't expect a gorilla to hold any Guinness World Records. *Inference AF3, AF5, AF6*
c. The word 'captivity' means being confined within a certain area. *Deduction AF3, AF5*
d. *Personal opinion AF2, AF3, AF5*

GO FOR GOLD!

a. Six of the zoo's gorillas are related to Colo. *Literal AF2*
b. The word 'endangered' means to be at risk of harm or extinction. *Inference AF3, AF5*
c. Colo has been important to the zoo because she is famous and brings visitors from other parts of the world. She has also successfully bred a large gorilla family. *Deduction AF3*
d. *Personal opinion AF2, AF3*

BEYOND THE RECORD

Use two sources to find out more about the life of Colo the gorilla and use the information to help you write a biography about her. Consider using photographs or a timeline.

Background research, reading and discussion to help the children to prepare

- Guide children to websites such as www.columbuszoo.org/, www.dispatch.com/content/stories/local/2012/12/22/animal-lovers-worldwide-go-ape-over-baby-colo.html and en.wikipedia.org/wiki/Colo_(gorilla).
- Discuss the features of a biography: structure of opening and closing statements with significant events in chronological order, dates, use of the past tense, written in the third person, time connectives, quotations, etc. Discuss who the biography could be aimed at, e.g. schools, zoo visitors, a newspaper.

Recording their ideas

- Encourage the children to decide how to record their ideas for their biography. Will they take notes while listening to a video, create a Mind Map™, create a timeline with notes and/or photographs?
- How will they create their biography? Will they create an oral presentation with a film, a Microsoft PowerPoint® presentation using photographs, videos and headlines, or a written text (an information text, a booklet, a leaflet for visitors)?

Ideas may include: Colo's birth, her parents, her early life in the zoo, special events, her family, her records, quotations from keepers and others.

LANGUAGE ACTIVITY WORKSHEET

- This worksheet allows children to revise the correct use of commas, semicolons, colons and capital letters for proper nouns. Explain to the children that they have to proofread the text carefully and add in the missing punctuation marks and capital letters. If appropriate, remind the children about the rules for using a semicolon and colon in texts. Encourage the children not to look at the text in the Pupil Book until they have finished.
- Once they have completed the proofreading, allow the children to self-mark using the original text from the Pupil Book.

NAME: DATE:

OFFICIALLY AMAZING

GLARING GORILLA MISTAKES!
Learning to proofread can help you to correct errors in your writing.

There are 10 missing punctuation marks and 12 missing capital letters in the text below. Proofread the text and correct the mistakes. Use the list at the bottom of the text to help you. Don't look at the original text until you have completed your work.

Colo the gorilla

The female gorilla colo has lived at the zoo all her life. Colo is a western lowland gorilla, and was born on 22 december 1956. Incredibly Colo holds two guinness world records she is the first ever gorilla born in captivity and at the age of 55 years, 11 months, 9 days as of 30 november 2012 she is the oldest living gorilla in captivity Colo has successfully bred a large gorilla family the zoo currently houses 15 gorillas six of which are related to colo.

Conservation

The columbus zoo and aquarium runs a conservation programme that helps to support conservation projects throughout the world. The programme has raised over $4 million in the last five years to support 70 projects in at least 30 countries worldwide. You can find out more about endangered species during your visit by reading the information provided with the exhibits. Donation boxes are also provided throughout the zoo.

1 semicolon (;)   1 colon (:)   12 capital letters for proper nouns   7 commas   1 full stop

© Rising Stars UK Ltd. 2013   Record-Breaking Comprehension/Year 6/First gorilla born in captivity

GUINNESS WORLD RECORDS

RECORD-BREAKING COMPREHENSION – YEAR 6

LARGEST MATCHSTICK MODEL

This magazine-style information text is about matchstick models. It focuses on the Guinness World Record for the largest matchstick model, which was made by David Reynolds.

Text type:	explanation/instruction
AFs covered:	AF2, AF3, AF5, AF6
Specialist vocabulary:	patience, engineer, structure, sculpture, success, painstaking

ON YOUR MARKS

a. The largest matchstick model was made from 4.075 million matchsticks. *Literal AF2*
b. David Reynolds made a model of a North Sea oil platform because he used to work on oil rigs. *Inference AF3*
c. You should be 'sparing' with the glue so that the matchsticks don't get over-sticky and make the model look messy. *Deduction AF3*
d. *Personal opinion AF2, AF3*

GET SET

a. The instruction is: 'To create curved sections, soak the matches in water overnight to make them easier to bend.' *Literal AF2*
b. 'Mastered the basics' means you have learned the main skills. You can then move on to more difficult skills. *Inference AF3, AF5*
c. The model had to be moved out of the Reynolds' house because it took up too much space. It was also less likely to get damaged in a museum. *Deduction AF3*
d. *Personal opinion AF2, AF3, AF6*

GO FOR GOLD!

a. Two imperative verbs used in the tips for success are 'cut' and 'clad'. *Literal AF2, AF5*
b. Matchstick modelling needs 'a great deal of patience' because it can take many hours of cutting and sticking small matchsticks to make a model. *Inference AF3, AF5*
c. A matchstick model structure may need more support because matchsticks are very thin and may not be able to hold the weight of the structure if a model is very large. *Deduction AF3*
d. *Personal opinion AF3*

BEYOND THE RECORD

Use books and the internet to search for four different matchstick models. Note down the key information about them. Use this information to create a page from a museum guide. What kind of information might a visitor to the museum want to know?

Background research, reading and discussion to help the children to prepare

- Provide a selection of hard-copy and online museum guides. See www.wonderfulinfo.com/arts/matchstick_armada/ or search Google Images for 'matchstick models'.
- Discuss what information the children need. What is the best way to present the information?

Recording their ideas

- Encourage the children to decide how to record their ideas. Will they use sticky notes, highlight information on a printed text, use key sub-headings with bullet points below?
- What presentational features will the children use to capture the visitors' attention?

Ideas may include: what the model is, who made it, how long it took, how many matches were used, information about the object that has been modelled.

LANGUAGE ACTIVITY WORKSHEET

- Use this worksheet to practise using bullet points within texts. Point to the information at the top of the page. Discuss with the children different examples of bullet points that they have seen in texts or used themselves. Emphasise the need for consistency when styling and punctuating bullets.
- The children should rewrite the relevant text in each paragraph as a bulleted list.
- They should complete the worksheet by writing one short example of a bulleted list.

Answers: It includes over: 10 scale miles of model railway track, 1.5 acres of beautiful gardens, over 200 amazingly detailed miniature model houses.

If you look hard enough you will see: the racecourse, the Manor House Hotel, the garden centre, the village morris dancers on the green, the hospital.

NAME: DATE:

MODELLING BULLET-POINT USE

Bullet points are used to list important information.

Bulleted lists should not be too long and should be consistent in design (dots, dashes, squares) and layout, e.g. all capitals or no capitals at the beginning of each bullet point, but not a mix.

Which part of these paragraphs can be written as bullet points?
Under each paragraph, write the relevant text as a bulleted list.

> Bekonscot Model Village and Railway is the famous model village in Beaconsfield in Buckinghamshire, which has been open to visitors since 1929. It includes over 10 scale miles of model railway track, 1.5 acres of beautiful gardens and over 200 amazingly detailed miniature model houses.

_____
_____
_____
_____

> One of the most popular attractions is a model village called Splashyng. If you look hard enough you will see the racecourse, the Manor House Hotel, the garden centre, the village morris dancers on the green and the hospital. It is so realistic that you almost believe that the people are real.

_____
_____
_____
_____
_____
_____

On the back of the worksheet, write one bulleted list connected to an interest or hobby that you have.

GUINNESS WORLD RECORDS
RECORD-BREAKING COMPREHENSION – YEAR 6

LARGEST VIOLIN

This page from an online encyclopedia provides information about the Guinness World Record for the largest violin and the area in Germany where it was made.

Text type:	non-chronological report
AFs covered:	AF2, AF3, AF4, AF5, AF6
Specialist vocabulary:	instrument, violin, replica, musician, harmonica, guild, guitar

ANSWERS

ON YOUR MARKS

a. Three people are needed to play the world's largest violin. *Literal AF2*
b. Two people are needed to move the bow because it is too long and awkward for one person to pull it across the strings. *Inference AF3*
c. Vogtland is called 'a musical place' because many musical instruments are made there. *Deduction AF3*
d. *Personal opinion AF2, AF3*

GET SET

a. Johann Georg Schönfelder II was famous for being a highly skilled violin maker and talented musician. *Literal AF2, AF6*
b. His violins are still popular because they were so well made and beautiful to look at. *Inference AF3, AF5*
c. '(1750–1824)' tells the reader the years when Johann Georg Schönfelder II was born and when he died. The numbers are in brackets because they are extra information and the sentence would work without the dates being there. *Deduction AF3, AF4*
d. *Personal opinion AF2, AF3, AF6*

GO FOR GOLD!

a. Johann Georg Schönfelder II's violins are described as 'exquisite golden-coloured violins'. *Literal AF2, AF5*
b. Violin and bow makers would want to live and work in Markneukirchen because they would be supported by the violin-making guild in making high-quality, beautiful violins. *Inference AF3*
c. The word 'exquisite' means very beautiful and delicate. *Inference AF3, AF5*
d. *Personal opinion AF3*

BEYOND THE RECORD

Use the internet to help you find out more information about Vogtland and Markneukirchen. Use the information to create a page from a travel brochure to persuade visitors to visit the region. Highlight the musical connections and history. Think about the layout and persuasive language you will use.

Background research, reading and discussion to help the children to prepare

- Collect and provide examples of travel brochures and visitor information leaflets.
- Guide children to websites such as www.markneukirchen.de/engl/tour/index.php, http://sachsen.de/en/258.htm and www.corilon.com/shop/en/info/markneukirchen.html.
- Discuss the persuasive features and layout of printed and online travel brochures. What does the reader need and want to know?

Recording their ideas

- How will the children choose and record the information for their travel page? Will they make notes under chosen headings, highlight printed text, create a Mind Map™?
- In what order will the children record their information? What layout will they use, and why? Will they include photographs? Why?

Ideas may include: where the region is, different reasons for people to visit (culture, music, beautiful scenery), brief history, eating and accommodation, museums, events.

LANGUAGE ACTIVITY WORKSHEET

- This worksheet looks at the rules for using semicolons. Give the worksheet to the children and point to the rules and examples on the page. If needed, look at a few more examples with the children before they start the worksheet.
- The children should plan a poster of the semicolon rules with their own examples. The poster can be used as a future reference tool for their writing. Check their examples to see if they have understood the rules correctly. Once their poster plans have been checked, the children can create the final poster.

NAME: **DATE:**

MUSICAL SEMICOLON POSTER

A semicolon (;) gives a sentence a slightly longer pause than a comma.

We use semicolons to connect two independent clauses that contain information relating to each other.

The violin was huge; it needed three people to play it.

We also use semicolons when we are joining two clauses using connective words such as otherwise, therefore, in addition, however.

I like listening to the violin; however, I don't like listening to the trumpet.

Plan a 'Using semicolons' poster that you can use for future writing work. Make sure you present the rules clearly and write a musical sentence example for each rule.

Rule 1:	Rule 2:
Example:	Example:

Check your work with your teacher before you create your poster.

GUINNESS WORLD RECORDS

RECORD-BREAKING COMPREHENSION – YEAR 6

LARGEST CONCENTRATION OF GEYSERS

This page from an encyclopedia provides information about geysers and how they work, and features famous geysers from Yellowstone National Park, which holds the Guinness World Record for the largest concentration of geysers.

Text type:	non-chronological report
AFs covered:	AF2, AF3, AF4, AF5, AF6
Specialist vocabulary:	geyser, intermittently, element, intense, pressure, concentration, plumbing, erupt

ON YOUR MARKS

a. Yellowstone Park lies mostly within the borders of Wyoming, USA. *Literal AF2*
b. 'Super-heated' means that something has been heated to an extremely hot temperature. *Inference AF3, AF5*
c. The list is numbered to show the reader the order of events leading to the eruption of a geyser. *Deduction AF3, AF4*
d. *Personal opinion AF2, AF3*

GET SET

a. A 'plumbing system' for a geyser is a set of tight rock channels that stop water rising easily to the surface. *Literal AF2, AF5*
b. Geysers are always found in active volcanic areas because the volcanic magma acts as a source of heat to raise the temperature of the underground water. *Inference AF3*
c. Tourists might 'flock to Yellowstone to watch the geysers' because there are many different types of geysers to see there. *Deduction AF3*
d. *Personal opinion AF2, AF6*

GO FOR GOLD!

a. The word rarity means 'uncommon' or 'unusual'. *Literal AF2, AF5*
b. 'A large amount of water' is needed to build up the pressure to create a geyser eruption. *Inference AF3, AF5*
c. Geysers are given specific names to emphasise the different ways they erupt. *Deduction AF3*
d. *Personal opinion AF4, AF6*

BEYOND THE RECORD

Use two sources to find out about the geysers at Yellowstone National Park. Create a presentation about one of the geysers to show to your class. Think about the use of clear, labelled diagrams, pictures, facts or film clips.

Background research, reading and discussion to help the children to prepare

- Research and choose a selection of video clips of Yellowstone geysers from sites such as www.yellowstone.co/videos/geysers/oldfaithful2.htm (more video clips can be found on YouTube).
- Guide children to websites such as www.yellowstonenationalpark.com and www.nps.gov/yell/naturescience/geysers.htm, and provide any other relevant resources containing scientific facts about how geysers are created.

Recording their ideas

- Encourage the children to decide on the type of presentation they are going to create, e.g. writing notes and diagrams on the whiteboard, narrating a film clip, creating a Microsoft PowerPoint® presentation.
- What presentational devices will they use?
- Is there a clear order of information in the presentation?

Feedback: Encourage the children to ask for feedback on their presentation. Did it have clear, concise information? Did it show a good understanding of the subject?

LANGUAGE ACTIVITY WORKSHEET

- Use the worksheet to look at the concept of cohesion within texts. If necessary, read through the text with the children and discuss the repeated and topic words that connect the text.
- Encourage the children to create their own text about a school trip using some of the words in the word box. Discuss how their recount has cohesion.

Answers: Science project, rocks and minerals, Blue John Cavern, caverns, visit, caverns, guide, limestone layers, embedded fossils, stalactites, stalagmites, rarest mineral, Blue John, leave, 9.30 am, back, 4.00 pm.

NAME: **DATE:**

COHESION OF TEXT

A text only makes sense if the words work together for the reader to understand its meaning or message.

We call this *cohesion*.

OFFICIALLY AMAZING

Underline repeated words and topic words that link the text's meaning. The first few are done for you.

> A <u>school trip</u> has been arranged for Willow and Oak class to <u>visit</u> the <u>Blue John Cavern</u>, near Castleton in Buxton, on 6 June as part of their science project on rocks and minerals. The Blue John Cavern is part of a series of caverns that are considered the best in Great Britain. During our visit, we will be exploring the caverns, with a guide, to study the clear limestone layers, the embedded fossils, to look at stalactites and stalagmites as well as to find out more about Britain's rarest mineral, Blue John. We plan to leave for the trip at 9.30 am and be back at school by 4.00 pm.

Write a recount of an imaginary school trip that uses some of the words in the box below.

_____
_____
_____
_____
_____
_____
_____

school trip   visit   Ancient Roman   history   project   Bath   hot spring
minerals   museum   ruins   hot baths   cool rooms   Britain   statues   gift shop

GUINNESS WORLD RECORDS

RECORD-BREAKING COMPREHENSION – YEAR 6

LARGEST PHOTO MOSAIC

This web page provides information about Guinness World Records Day, when people all over the world attempt to set or break a record. The text recounts the seventh GWR Day when a team from Japan created a record-breaking photo mosaic.

Text type:	non-chronological report/recount
AFs covered:	AF2, AF3, AF4, AF5, AF6
Specialist vocabulary:	mosaic, photograph, memorable, application, imaginative, Japanese

ON YOUR MARKS

a. On Guinness World Records Day, people from all over the world attempt to set new records or break existing records. *Literal AF2*

b. People want to attempt a Guinness World Record for several reasons, such as being in the record books, achieving something remarkable, or doing something fun and original. *Deduction AF3*

c. This paragraph is about what to do if you want to take part in Guinness World Records Day. *Inference AF3, AF4, AF6*

d. *Personal opinion AF3*

GET SET

a. In Bologna, Italy, on 15 November 2012, the Guinness World Record was broken for the largest chocolate coin. *Literal AF2*

b. The word 'adjudicator' means someone who judges or makes an official decision about something. *Inference AF3, AF5*

c. The adjudicator needs to check that the record attempt is 'done properly' to make sure that the rules of the record are followed and that the record is broken fairly. *Deduction AF3, AF4*

d. *Personal opinion AF2, AF3*

GO FOR GOLD!

a. The photo mosaic was made from photographs of pets because the team who made it worked for a pet store. *Literal AF2*

b. Some records were 'memorable' because they were very unusual and people would remember them. *Inference AF3, AF5*

c. The opening sentence is a question to encourage the reader to think about what kind of Guinness World Record they would like to attempt. *Deduction AF3, AF4, AF6*

d. *Personal opinion AF3*

BEYOND THE RECORD

Use the Guinness World Records website to select your favourite three records. Create a PowerPoint® presentation explaining what they are. Share your presentation with others in your class and discuss why you chose the three records.

Background research, reading and discussion to help the children to prepare

- Guide children to the Guinness World Records website: www.guinnessworldrecords.com/.
- With the children, discuss the kind of information they will use for their presentation.

Recording their ideas

- How will the children work? Individually, in pairs or as small groups? If in pairs or groups, how will they decide on their records – through discussion, voting, by debate?
- What presentational devices will the children use to help them structure their presentation? Bullet points, photographs, headings, sub-headings? Encourage feedback after the presentations.

LANGUAGE ACTIVITY WORKSHEET

- Use the worksheet to look at how hyphens can be used to avoid ambiguity. Point to the definition and example at the top of the worksheet. Discuss how the first sentence could be confusing without the use of a hyphen.
- Once the children have completed the worksheet, encourage them to research more examples of hyphenation.

NAME: DATE:

HYPHEN MOSAIC

Sometimes two words next to each other can have two different meanings and confuse the reader when put in a sentence.

We can use hyphens (-) to make the meaning clear.

The little used bike was thrown in the skip.
The little-used bike was a perfect present for Joe.

Write a sentence to show the meaning of the pairs of unhyphenated and hyphenated words and phrases below. The first one has been done for you.

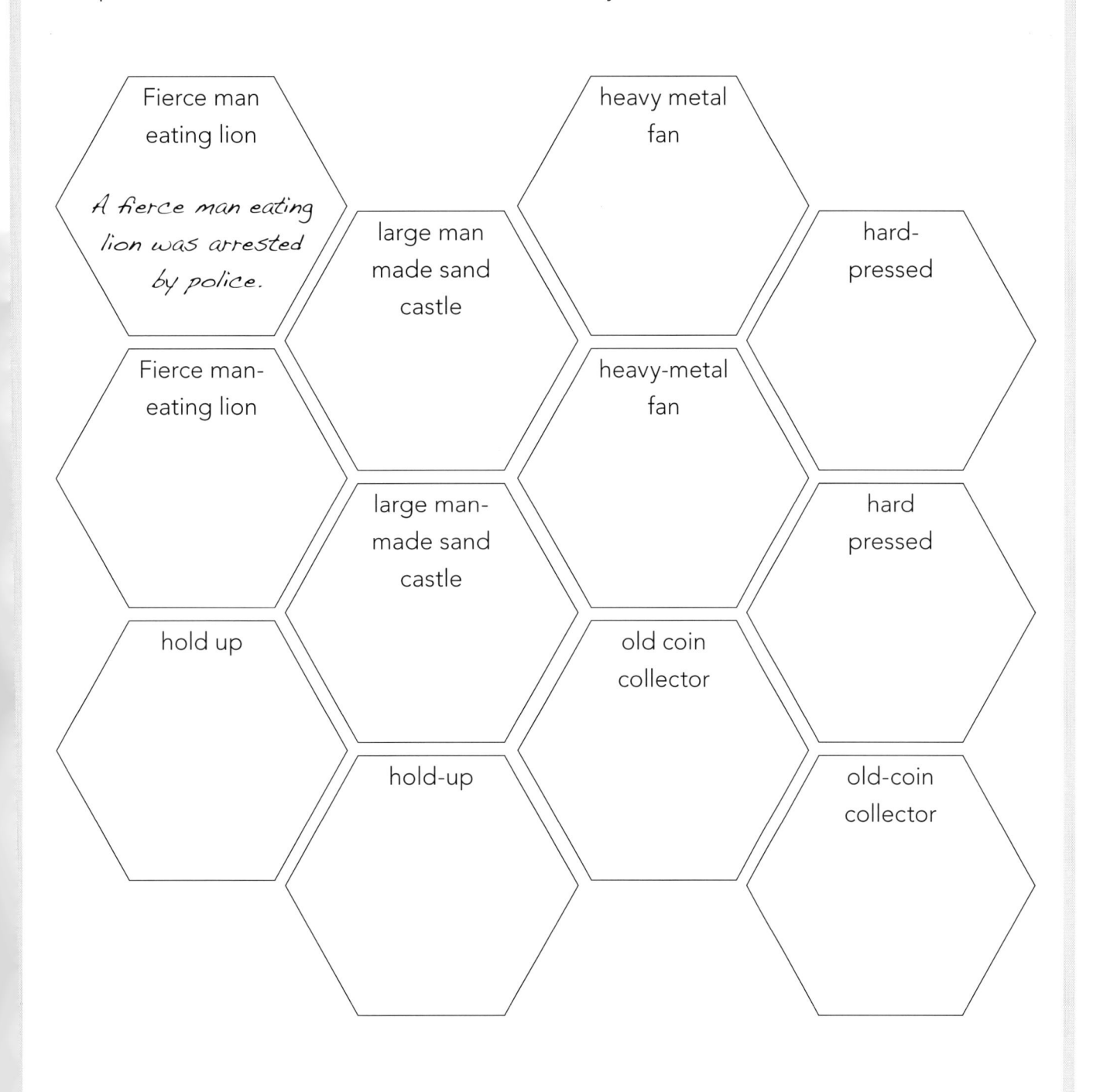

- Fierce man eating lion

  A fierce man eating lion was arrested by police.

- large man made sand castle
- heavy metal fan
- hard-pressed
- Fierce man-eating lion
- heavy-metal fan
- large man-made sand castle
- hard pressed
- hold up
- old coin collector
- hold-up
- old-coin collector

GUINNESS WORLD RECORDS

RECORD-BREAKING COMPREHENSION – YEAR 6

MOST CONSECUTIVE FOOT-JUGGLING FLIPS

This gymnastics newsletter text is about Hou Yanan and Jiang Tiantian, who together broke the Guinness World Record for the most consecutive foot-juggling flips.

Text type:	recount
AFs covered:	AF2, AF3, AF4, AF5, AF6
Specialist vocabulary:	consecutive, accuracy, somersault, juggling, discipline, acrobat

ON YOUR MARKS

a. Hou and Jiang belong to the Chinese Wuqiao County Aerobatic Group. *Literal AF2*
b. The judges were 'looking on' to check that each of the foot-juggling flips were performed correctly. *Inference AF3*
c. A 'sloped padded stool' would help support the legs and back of the acrobat who was juggling the second acrobat, and ensure that she was comfortable during the record attempt. *Deduction AF3*
d. *Personal opinion AF2, AF3*

GET SET

a. Wuqiao County is famous for producing and training the best acrobats in China. *Literal AF2*
b. Pupils start training when they are young so that they have more time to practise acrobatic moves and become skilled acrobats. *Inference AF3*
c. The title of the article uses alliteration (foot, flipping, feat). The writer also uses the homophones 'feat' and 'feet'. These features grab the reader's attention. *Deduction AF3, AF4, AF6*
d. *Personal opinion AF2, AF3*

GO FOR GOLD!

a. Chinese acrobats have skill and discipline. *Literal AF2, AF4*
b. The writer uses adjectives such as 'remarkable' and 'incredible'. *Inference AF3, AF5*
c. 'Feat' means a remarkable achievement and is linked to the homphone 'feet'. 'Propelled' means to be pushed forward, and is linked to the acrobats' moves. *Deduction AF3, AF5, AF6*
d. *Personal opinion AF2, AF3*

BEYOND THE RECORD

Imagine you are interviewing Hou Yanan and Jiang Tiantian after their record attempt. Write down five questions that you would like to ask them about the record attempt and how they prepared for it. Role-play the interview, taking it in turns to ask your questions to the 'acrobats'.

Background research, reading and discussion to help the children to prepare

- As well as using the Pupil Book text, look at online information about Chinese acrobatics, e.g. www.circopedia.org/index.php/The_Chinese_Acrobatic_Theater.
- Guide children to the Wuqiao acrobatic school website: www.admissions.cn/wqzj/index.html.
- If possible, show a video clip of acrobats performing foot-juggling flips (see YouTube).

Recording their ideas

- How will the children select their questions? Will they ask questions about the acrobats' backgrounds? Or will their questions be mainly focused on the record attempt?
- During the role-play activity, encourage the children to consider whether the questions allow the acrobats to impart interesting views and information about the record attempt.

LANGUAGE ACTIVITY WORKSHEET

- Use this worksheet to help reinforce learning the spellings and difference in meaning of difficult homophones. Remind the children what a homophone is and give a few examples.
- First, the children should insert the correct homophones into the headlines. Then ask them to think of a strategy to help them remember various homophones. Each pair could have a different cue, e.g. visual, rhyme.
- Encourage the children to write a couple more headlines using homophones. Do their strategies work?

Answers: (from left to right) alter/altar, allowed/aloud, serial/cereal, morning/mourning, assent/ascent, bridle/bridal, stationery/stationary.

| NAME: | DATE: |

HOMOPHONE HEADLINE PUNS

Homophones are words that are spelled differently and have different meanings, but sound the same.

feat: a remarkable achievement or act.
feet: the lower parts of the legs used for standing and walking.

Write the correct homophones in the headlines using the words in the box.

OUTRAGE AS VICAR PLANS TO _____ THE RARE _____

SECRET PAPERS _____ TO BE READ

EXCITING NEW ADVENTURE _____ AS YOU EAT YOUR _____

A tragic _____ of deep _____

Ruler gives _____ for record attempt of mountain _____

Brave bride snatches _____ from scared horse in her _____ gown

Striking staff at _____ shop stay _____

---

father	stationary	bridle	serial	mourning	steel
assent	aloud	morning	alter	bridal	cereal	ascent
stationery	farther	steal	altar	allowed

Write two of your own headlines using the four remaining homophones.

_____

_____

GUINNESS WORLD RECORDS

RECORD-BREAKING COMPREHENSION – YEAR 6

LARGEST PANORAMIC PAINTING

This arts and crafts magazine article explains how to create a panoramic painting, and also highlights the Guinness World Record for the largest panoramic painting, created in China in 2011.

Text type:	recount/instructions
AFs covered:	AF2, AF3, AF4, AF5, AF6
Specialist vocabulary:	panoramic, technique, landscape, sketch, canvas, photograph

ON YOUR MARKS

a. The record-breaking panoramic painting was called 'Splendid Central Plains'. *Literal AF2*
b. Thirteen painters were needed to paint the largest panoramic painting because it was so long. *Inference AF3*
c. You would need to take sketches or photographs to help you record the view and link the different sections together when painting the panorama. *Deduction AF3*
d. *Personal opinion AF3*

GET SET

a. The world's largest panoramic painting is 163.52 m long and 18.422 m wide. *Literal AF2*
b. The word 'panoramic' means the full view of a scene or events. *Inference AF3, AF5*
c. The instructions in the text are numbered to help the reader follow the steps in the correct order. *Deduction AF3, AF4, AF6*
d. *Personal opinion AF2, AF3*

GO FOR GOLD!

a. The time connectives used in the text are 'next', 'after', 'finally' (any two of these answers are acceptable). *Literal AF2, AF4*
b. You need to slowly scan your chosen view so that you can take in as much detail and information as possible. *Inference AF3*
c. People from the Henan Province would want to see the largest panoramic painting because it would show some of the landmarks and landscape of their country. *Deduction AF3*
d. *Personal opinion AF3*

BEYOND THE RECORD

Use the internet and art books to study some examples of panoramic paintings and photographs. Choose one panoramic painting or photograph and write interesting information about it for visitors to an art exhibition. How can you make the visitors look more closely at the picture?

Background research, reading and discussion to help the children to prepare

- Provide a range of art books that feature panoramic paintings and/or photographs.
- As a class, search for panoramic images on the internet (type 'panorama' into a Google Image search).
- Discuss what an exhibition visitor would want to know when looking at a panoramic picture: its name, where or what it shows, points of interest. Emphasise the need for clear and concise information and persuasive vocabulary.

Recording their ideas

- Encourage the children to select a panoramic picture and decide how to record the information they will need. Will they use sticky notes, lists, a Mind Map™, sub-headings with bullets?
- How will they structure their information? Sub-headings with bullets summarising information, or paragraphs?

Other ideas: Put on a mini art exhibition of the panoramic pictures with the children's visitor information underneath. Which information is eye-catching and clear to read? Does the information make you want to look more closely at the picture?

LANGUAGE ACTIVITY WORKSHEET

- This worksheet allows the children to practise proofreading a text for spelling mistakes. Explain that 10 of the words have been spelled incorrectly. Ask the children to proofread the text carefully and underline the incorrect words. They should rewrite the words correctly at the bottom of the worksheet.
- Allow the children to use word banks or dictionaries to help them, if required. Once they have completed the proofreading, ask them to self-mark using the original text.

Answers: Panoramic, huge, battle, artists, techniques, popular, historical, Administration, Television, landscapes.

PANORAMIC PROOFREADING

Proofreading your work can help you to correct spelling mistakes.

There are 10 spelling mistakes in the text below. Read through the text and underline the wrong spellings. Write the correct spellings at the bottom of the page. Use a dictionary if you need help.

> Panoremic paintings are hug artworks that show a full view of something such as a landscape, a city, a battel or an event. They can take many months, even years, of work with several artests painting different sections of the view at the same time. Panoramic painting tecniques were particularly poplar in the mid-19th century, and were created to show landscapes or historcal events.
>
> On 26 April 2011, a panoramic painting called 'Splendid Central Plains' was unveiled by the Henan Adminstraton of Radio Film and Televison (China) at the Tower of Fortune in Zhengzhou City, Henan Province, China.
>
> Working on a 163.52-m-long and 18.422-m-wide canvas, 13 painters took 345 days to paint a panoramic view of the landscaps and landmarks of the Henan province. The finished panoramic painting measured 3,012.365 m² (nearly 2 miles!), breaking the Guinness World Record for largest panoramic painting.

When you have finished, use the original text to check your work. Did you find all of the spelling mistakes?

GUINNESS WORLD RECORDS

RECORD-BREAKING COMPREHENSION – YEAR 6

LONGEST TIME TO LIVE WITH A BULLET IN THE HEAD

This magazine text tells the life story of William Lawlis Pace, from the USA, who on 20 July 2006 broke the Guinness World Record for the longest time to live with a bullet in the head.

Text type:	biography
AFs covered:	AF2, AF3, AF4, AF5, AF6
Specialist vocabulary:	bullet, facial, cemetery, courageously, accidentally, celebrity

ON YOUR MARKS

a. William Lawlis Pace was born in Wheeler, Texas, USA. *Literal AF2*

b. Pace's long life was 'remarkable' because he lived a long and full life after an accident during his childhood left him with a bullet lodged in his head. *Inference AF3, AF5*

c. Pace needed to have an X-ray as this was the only safe way to prove that a bullet was in his head and that he had broken the Guinness World Record. *Deduction AF3*

d. *Personal opinion AF3*

GET SET

a. The bullet was not taken out of Pace's head because an operation could have caused serious brain damage. *Literal AF2*

b. It was brave for Pace to be a catcher in baseball because his head could have been hurt further if hit by a baseball. *Inference AF3*

c. The text is a biography. It is recounting the life of someone. *Deduction AF3, AF4*

d. *Personal opinion AF2, AF5, AF6*

GO FOR GOLD!

a. William's family believed he survived because of 'his hard-working and happy nature'. *Literal AF2*

b. The author used the word 'courageously' to describe Pace's efforts to continue a normal life despite his disabilities. *Inference AF3, AF5*

c. Pace wanted to carry on as normal after the accident because he was a hard-working and happy person who didn't want his disabilities to get in the way of day-to-day activities. *Deduction AF3*

d. *Personal opinion AF2, AF3*

BEYOND THE RECORD

Choose a famous person from the past. Use the internet to find out more information about them and write three paragraphs to summarise their life. Ask someone else to review your work. Does it sum up their life in an interesting way?

Background research, reading and discussion to help the children to prepare

- Guide children to biographical websites such as www.bbc.co.uk/history/historic_figures/a.shtml.
- Briefly discuss the features of a biography.
- Discuss what *summarise* means. Explain that the children need to present the information in the three paragraphs in an interesting way.

Recording their ideas

- How will the children present their three paragraphs? Will they use sub-headings, underlining, different fonts, short and effective sentences, bullet points, memorable vocabulary?

Feedback: Do their paragraphs show biographical features? Ask the children to discuss their methods of taking notes and summarising the information.

LANGUAGE ACTIVITY WORKSHEET

- Use the worksheet to consolidate skills on expanded noun phrases. Discuss why expanded noun phrases can make writing more interesting.
- Explain that books often include a blurb (short description) on the back cover to give readers an idea of what the book is about. The children must identify and underline examples of expanded noun phrases in three book blurbs. They then have to create two more of their own.
- If some children struggle with the extension task, highlight some of their text and support them to add noun phrases.

Answers: Sweet memories, amusing aunt, lived on a barge; speedy van man, the man who can; spine-chilling account, life of a ghost hunter.

NAME: DATE:

BOOK BLURB NOUN PHRASES

An expanded noun phrase is a word or group of words that adds extra information to the main noun. We use them to make our writing more interesting and vivid for the reader.

We can add different words before or after the noun such as adjectives, pronouns, prepositions, verbs and adverbs.

noun = frog   <u>A slimy, green frog</u> with <u>diamond and ruby eyes</u>.

Underline the expanded noun phrases in the blurbs. Then write two of your own expanded-noun-phrase blurbs in the space provided.

Sweet memories of an amusing aunt, who lived on a barge

SPEEDY VAN MAN, DAN, IS THE MAN WHO CAN

THE SPINE-CHILLING ACCOUNT OF THE LIFE OF A GHOST HUNTER

Choose one of the characters or objects above and write a fictional paragraph about them/it. Include some expanded noun phrases to make the text more interesting for the reader.

_____
_____
_____
_____
_____
_____
_____

GUINNESS WORLD RECORDS

RECORD-BREAKING COMPREHENSION – YEAR 6

LONGEST DISTANCE RUN FULL-BODY BURN (WITHOUT OXYGEN)

This blog-style recount text is written about Ted Batchelor, who broke the Guinness World Record for the longest distance running while on fire.

Text type:	recount
AFs covered:	AF2, AF3, AF5, AF6
Specialist vocabulary:	oxygen, atmosphere, experience, fiery, intensely, achievement

ON YOUR MARKS

a. Ted Batchelor performs stunts involving fire. *Literal AF2*
b. 'The whole place had gone mad' means that the crowd was very excited watching Ted Batchelor perform his stunt. *Inference AF3, AF5, AF6*
c. The crowd was screaming because Ted Batchelor was performing a very dangerous stunt and could have been seriously hurt if it went wrong. *Deduction AF3, AF5*
d. Harvey includes a safety notice to remind people not to try to recreate the stunt because it is very dangerous. *Deduction AF3*

GET SET

a. Joe and Harvey squeezed through a gap in the crowd to the safety barrier. *Literal AF2*
b. Harvey wanted to catch a glimpse of Ted Batchelor running past while on fire, which would have felt hot. *Inference AF3, AF5*
c. The safety barriers were put up to protect the crowd from the fire and to give Ted Batchelor a clear run without any obstacles. *Deduction AF3*
d. *Personal opinion AF3, AF6*

GO FOR GOLD!

a. Harvey calls Ted Batchelor 'Man on Fire'. *Literal AF2*
b. The phrase 'soaking up the atmosphere' means that Harvey was enjoying the feeling of the Christmas celebrations going on around him. *Inference AF3, AF5*
c. Harvey's blog audience is likely to be his family and friends, who he knows well. *Deduction AF3, AF6*
d. *Personal opinion AF3*

BEYOND THE RECORD

Imagine that Ted is coming to your school to give a talk about his fire stunts and world records. With a partner, or on your own, write a list of six questions that you would like to ask him. Use these questions in a hot-seating drama activity with a partner.

Background research, reading and discussion to help the children to prepare

- As a class, look at Ted Batchelor's website: http://tedbatchelor.com/. Discuss the information and video clips available.
- Make sure the children have access to the text from the Pupil Book.

Recording their ideas

- Encourage the children to decide how to record their ideas for questions. Will they use sticky notes, highlight parts of the text that they want to ask questions about, create a Mind Map™?
- How will they select the best questions? Do they have a good mix of questions that cover a range of points? Are the questions open or closed?
- After the hot-seating drama activity, did the children think that they had chosen the right questions? Did they want to ask more questions about one area, such as Ted's safety or why he performs fire stunts?

Ideas for questions may include: his life, his motives for being a stuntman, his best stunt or record attempt, a stunt or record attempt he wouldn't want to do again, the dangers of being a stuntman.

LANGUAGE ACTIVITY WORKSHEET

- Use the worksheet to introduce or revise work on adverbial phrases. Explain how adverbial phrases can be used and look at the four examples at the top of the page. Discuss how the adverbial phrases make a difference to each basic sentence.
- Ask the children to use adverbial phrases to improve the two simple sentences given. Discuss their choice of phrases.
- Allow the children to share their own sentences. How have adverbial phrases improved the sentences?

NAME: _____ DATE: _____

ADVERBIAL STUNT ACTIONS

We use adverbial phrases to add extra detail by explaining *how, when, where* and *why*.

The stuntman ran could be changed to:

The intrepid stuntman ran <u>quickly out of the exploding building</u>. (how)
<u>A few minutes ago</u>, the terrified stuntman ran away. (when)
The brave stuntman ran <u>off the edge of a tall building</u>. (where)
The tired stuntman ran <u>because he was being chased by a car</u>. (why)

For each sentence below, write four new sentences by adding details for *how, when, where* and *why*.

Use an adjective in front of the noun to make your writing more interesting.

The stuntwoman fell.

1. _____
2. _____
3. _____
4. _____

The stunt dog danced.

1. _____
2. _____
3. _____
4. _____

Write a simple sentence of your choice. Then write four new sentences using adverbial phrases (how, when, where, why).

1. _____
2. _____
3. _____
4. _____

GUINNESS WORLD RECORDS

RECORD-BREAKING COMPREHENSION – YEAR 6

OLDEST SCULPTURE

This online encyclopedia text on sculpture includes information about a bone carving that is recognised by Guinness World Records as the oldest sculpture.

Text type:	non-chronological report
AFs covered:	AF2, AF3, AF4, AF5, AF6
Specialist vocabulary:	sculpture, archaeologist, prehistoric, artefact, evidence, vertebra

ON YOUR MARKS

a. The world's oldest known sculpture is a head of a bear carved onto a piece of backbone from a prehistoric woolly rhinoceros. *Literal AF2*

b. Most early sculptures were small because they were created from small bits of material, such as stone, wood, horn and tusk. *Inference AF3*

c. 'A range of materials' means different types of material. *Deduction AF3, AF4*

d. Personal opinion *AF4*

GET SET

a. The world's oldest sculpture was found along the banks of the Khilok River near the town of Tolbaga in Siberia, Russia. *Literal AF2*

b. Early sculptures were mostly carved from wood, bone, stone and tusks as these materials were the easiest to find. *Inference AF3*

c. An 'artefact' is an object with cultural or historical importance, which has been made by humans. *Deduction AF3, AF5*

d. Personal opinion *AF3*

GO FOR GOLD!

a. No early wooden carvings have been found because they have rotted away. *Literal AF2*

b. Many artefacts have been found in caves and near river banks because these places are probably where early humans lived. *Inference AF3*

c. It is important to carbon-date artefacts so that we can find out how long ago humans lived and what they were doing at that time. *Deduction AF3*

d. Personal opinion *AF3, AF6*

BEYOND THE RECORD

Use two sources to find out more about other sculptures that hold a Guinness World Record, such as the largest chocolate sculpture, the longest sand sculpture, or the largest scrap metal sculpture. Choose your favourite and write down five bullet points to summarise why you like it.

Background research, reading and discussion to help the children to prepare

- Provide copies of the Guinness World Records book, or guide children to the Guinness World Records website: www.guinnessworldrecords.com/.
- Discuss the challenges of summarising information as bullet points: only key ideas should be presented.

Recording their ideas

- How will children select key information about the record they choose? Will they highlight key information in a text or write draft bullet points to be edited later?
- How will the children condense and refine the information into bullet points?

LANGUAGE ACTIVITY WORKSHEET

- This worksheet reviews work on the use of colons. Explain that a colon is used by writers to create a stronger division within a sentence. Discuss why a colon should not always be used and what types of text lend themselves more to using them, e.g. information texts or dramatic points in a narrative.
- Check the children's work to see if they have understood how to use colons. Point out the independent clause before the lists.
- Encourage children to share their finished piece with others. Have they used colons correctly? Are they used effectively?

Answers: 1. colon before *temperature*, 2. colon before *they*, 3. colon before *it*, 4. colon before *material*; 1. colon before *a shovel*, 2. colon before *stone*.

SCULPTURING TEXT WITH COLONS

Colons are used to make a stronger, more effective separation of two clauses in a sentence.
The first clause must make sense on its own.
The second clause follows on with an explanation or a statement of a fact about the first clause.

The huge sculpture was made from my favourite food: chocolate!
All the sculptures have one similar feature: they are made of bone.

Add the missing colons in the sentences below.

1. Ice sculptors are constantly aware of one thing while they are sculpting the temperature.
2. There are many ice-sculpting events around the world they tend to be in countries with cold winters.
3. In 2012, I saw a sand sculpture of Queen Elizabeth II it was for her Diamond Jubilee.
4. Native American Indians created totem poles out of one type of material wood.

You can also use a colon at the beginning of a list. Make sure the clause before the list makes sense on its own.

I love three types of sculptures: totem poles, stone sculptures and ice sculptures.

Add colons to the lists below.

1. To make a sand sculpture you need four things a shovel, buckets, a casting bucket and your hands!
2. Most prehistoric sculptures were made from five materials stone, bone, horn, wood and ivory tusks.

On the back of this sheet, write a short piece about a sculpture. Include one or more colons in the text.

GUINNESS WORLD RECORDS
RECORD-BREAKING COMPREHENSION – YEAR 6

LARGEST MEDICINAL HERB GARDEN

This magazine article includes information about the Guangxi Botanical Garden of Medicinal Plants in China, which is recognised by Guinness World Records as the largest medicinal herb garden.

Text type:	non-chronological report
AFs covered:	AF2, AF3, AF4, AF6
Specialist vocabulary:	medicinal, remedies, traditional, herbal, alternative, chemicals

ON YOUR MARKS

a. Roots, bark, leaves or flowers can be used to create medicines. *Literal AF2*

b. People in the past took herbal medicines to help them recover from illnesses because herbal medicines were all that were available at the time. *Inference AF3*

c. Herb plants are seen as healthier than man-made drugs because they are not made from man-made chemicals. *Deduction AF3*

d. Personal opinion *AF3*

GET SET

a. The garden staff have collected approximately 100,000 ancient and modern pictures of medicinal plants. *Literal AF2*

b. The garden protects the future of medicinal herb plants by growing them in a protected place, where they cannot be picked, and storing thousands of their seeds. *Inference AF3*

c. The author wants us to feel that the garden is an important and special place because the staff that work there are ensuring endangered plant species survive. *Deduction AF3, AF6*

d. Personal opinion *AF3, AF6*

GO FOR GOLD!

a. The connective phrases are: 'In the past'; 'As time passed'; 'The exception to this is'; 'Luckily'; 'Since it opened'; 'As a result' (any two of these answers are acceptable). *Literal AF2, AF4*

b. The world's largest medicinal herb garden is in China because many of its population still use traditional medicinal herbs every day. *Inference AF3*

c. Ancient and modern pictures of medicinal plants can help gardeners and scientists identify rare and endangered plants so that they can protect them from extinction. *Deduction AF3*

d. Personal opinion *AF3*

BEYOND THE RECORD

Choose two sources to find out about medicinal herbs and flowers that grow in Britain (examples are mint, chickweed and dandelions). Select one plant and make notes on its habitat, what it looks like and what it can be used for.

Background research, reading and discussion to help the children to prepare

- Show the children books, leaflets, posters and images relating to medicinal herbs and flowers.
- Guide children to websites such as www.herbsociety.org.uk.
- Stress that not all herbs and flowers are medicinal and safe to eat and that children should never pick and eat a wild plant without checking with an adult first.

Recording their ideas

- How will the children record their ideas? Using sticky notes, lists, sub-headings, by highlighting interesting information?
- How will they present their findings? A labelled diagram, clear paragraphs, bulleted lists, images?

Ideas may include: common and Latin name, history of medicinal use, habitat, care, medicinal parts, preparation, other uses such as cooking.

LANGUAGE ACTIVITY WORKSHEET

- Point out the words *herbal* and *medicinal* in the Pupil Book text and discuss their meaning in relation to the text. Discuss the suffix *-al* and its usage.
- Ask the children to list words ending with *-al*. Discuss the spelling patterns and meanings.
- Fast finishers can create sentences using four *-al* words of their choice. Do the sentences make sense?

Possible answers: musical, comical, diabolical, ethical, unequivocal, classical, logical, fictional, educational, clinical.

NAME: DATE:

HERBAL SUFFIXES

The word *herbal* uses the suffix *-al*, which means 'relating to'.
herb = herb + al = herbal
(If the root word ends in *e*, drop the *e* before adding *–al*.)
medicine +al = medicinal

Using a dictionary to help you, list words that end with the suffix *-al*.

How many can you find?

Write your words here.

Use your *-al* words to create four sentences.

1. _____
2. _____
3. _____
4. _____

NOTES

Use this page to make notes about the reading comprehension texts and activities or any topic/subject links with your curriculum to share with other class teachers.